TOWARD CULTURALLY SUSTAINING TEACHING

Demonstrating equitable practices and strategies that move toward culturally sustaining teaching such as translanguaging, explorations of children's literature, alternative modes of literacy assessment, photography and arts integration, student-driven poetry units, and more, this book shares the stories of four teacher–teacher dyads who worked together across university–school contexts to study, generate, and evaluate culturally relevant and sustaining literacy practices in early childhood classrooms across the country. Highlighting the voices and roles of children, families, community members, and teachers of Color, this book suggests new ways for all teachers to build and sustain relationships that are relevant and work toward being sustaining; and anticipates and offers solutions for challenges that arise in these contexts. Insightful and instructive, the narratives in this collection model how to create positive and mutually beneficial dynamics among teachers, children, and their families and communities.

This book offers a timely resource for preservice teachers, teachers, scholars, faculty, and graduate students in language and literacy education, early childhood education, and culturally relevant, responsive, and sustaining teaching.

Kindel Turner Nash is an Associate Professor of Early Childhood Education at the University of Maryland, Baltimore County, USA.

Crystal Polite Glover is an Assistant Professor of Early Childhood Education at Winthrop University, USA.

Bilal Polson is the Principal of Northern Parkway School in Uniondale, New York, USA.

NCTE-ROUTLEDGE RESEARCH SERIES

Series Editors: Valerie Kinloch and Susi Long

Daniell/Mortensen
Women and Literacy: Local and Global Inquiries for a New Century

Rickford/Sweetland/Rickford/ Grano
African American, Creole and other Vernacular Englishes in Education: A Bibliographic Resource

Guerra
Language, Culture, Identity, and Citizenship in College Classrooms and Communities

Haddix
Cultivating Racial and Linguistic Diversity in Literacy Teacher Education: Teachers Like Me

Brooks
Transforming Literacy Education for Long-Term English Learners: Recognizing Brilliance in the Undervalued

Baker-Bell
Linguistic Justice: Black Language, Literacy, Identity, and Pedagogy

Nash, Polson, Glover
Toward Culturally Sustaining Teaching: Early Childhood Educators Honor Children with Practices for Equity and Change

The NCTE-Routledge Research Series, copublished by the National Council of Teachers of English and Routledge, focuses on literacy studies in P-12 classroom and related contexts. Volumes in this series are invited publications or publications submitted in response to a call for manuscripts. They are primarily authored or co-authored works which are theoretically significant and broadly relevant to the P-12 literacy community. The series may also include occasional landmark compendiums of research.

The scope of the series includes qualitative and quantitative methodologies; a range of perspectives and approaches (e.g., sociocultural, cognitive, feminist, linguistic, pedagogical, critical, historical, anthropological); and research on diverse populations, contexts (e.g., classrooms, school systems, families, communities), and forms of literacy (e.g., print, electronic, popular media).

TOWARD CULTURALLY SUSTAINING TEACHING

Early Childhood Educators Honor Children with Practices for Equity and Change

Edited by Kindel Turner Nash, Crystal Polite Glover, and Bilal Polson

NEW YORK AND LONDON

First published 2021
by Routledge
52 Vanderbilt Avenue, New York, NY 10017

and by Routledge
2 Park Square, Milton Park, Abingdon, Oxon OX14 4RN

Routledge is an imprint of the Taylor & Francis Group, an informa business

Library of Congress Cataloging-in-Publication Data
Names: Nash, Kindel A. Turner, editor. | Glover, Crystal Polite, 1974- editor. | Polson, Bilal, editor.
Title: Toward culturally sustaining teaching : early childhood educators honor children with practices for equity and change / edited by Kindel Nash, Crystal Glover and Bilal Polson.
Description: New York, NY : Routledge, 2020. | Series: NCTE-Routledge research series | Includes bibliographical references and index. |
Identifiers: LCCN 2019058857 (print) | LCCN 2019058858 (ebook) | ISBN 9780815363750 (hardback) | ISBN 9780815363774 (paperback) | ISBN 9781351108317 (ebook)
Subjects: LCSH: Culturally relevant pedagogy--United States. | Early childhood education--Social aspects--United States. | Language arts (Early childhood)--United States.
Classification: LCC LC1099.3 .T67 2020 (print) | LCC LC1099.3 (ebook) | DDC 370.117--dc23
LC record available at https://lccn.loc.gov/2019058857
LC ebook record available at https://lccn.loc.gov/2019058858

ISBN: 978-0-815-36375-0 (hbk)
ISBN: 978-0-815-36377-4 (pbk)
ISBN: 978-1-351-10831-7 (ebk)

Typeset in Bembo
by Taylor & Francis Books

Visit the eresources at: http://www.routledge.com/9780815363750

We dedicate this book to the teachers, children, families, and communities we are so humbled to learn from every day. Theirs are the voices, experiences, and lives we hope to honor in this volume.

CONTENTS

FIGURES

TABLES

SERIES FOREWORD

> *One day in mid-March, Kindel arrived at Patricia's classroom to find Patricia very upset.* [Three-year-old] *Santiago, fluent speaker of Spanish, had just failed the language articulation portion of the DIAL-IV assessment which had been administered in English by a testing administrator who was a district special education coordinator and a stranger to Santiago. Patricia explained Santiago's testing encounter:*
>
> *You know, [the children] don't feel comfortable sometimes with the strangers. So, he got zero on the language part of test* [the part that orally assesses first/last name, age, day, month, year as well as phonemic awareness]. *I told the lady that he should not have failed, he definitely knew his name and age and he could say most of his letters. I tried to show them his portfolio.*

Santiago's story is at the heart of this book's commitment to counter, dismantle, and replace injustices in the teaching and assessment of children most marginalized and silenced in schools and society. Knowing Santiago in a caring context that assumed expertise and valued his cultural and linguistic knowledge, it would have been obvious that he was well aware of phonemes, his name, and his age. It is for every Santiago that we join this book's co-editors—Kindel Nash, Crystal Glover, and Bilal Polson—in sharing the work of teachers and teacher educators who engage in oppositional teaching to that which dismissed the possibility that Santiago was knowledgeable and skilled. This kind of culturally relevant teaching is at the heart of the book's commitment to "transformational love and education for the human soul," words from educator-activist Anna Julia Cooper which open the volume.

Moving beyond typical reporting of research and practice, the first chapter of *Toward Culturally Sustaining Teaching: Early Childhood Educators Honor Children with Practices for Equity and Change* offers a discussion of the "family tree" that guides the authors' work. Not just a focus on a review of research, the tree lovingly emphasizes lessons from antiracist movements and activists across time, highlighting generations of resistance to Eurocratic schooling that continues to dehumanize children. Subsequent chapters focus on day-to-day life in the classrooms of children from pre-kindergarten through fourth grade as authors insist that antiracist, humanizing, culturally relevant teaching must begin with our youngest children. The closing chapter draws out lessons for teachers and teacher educators, urging all of us to take up the challenge for change. Throughout, we are urged to consider when culturally relevant teaching becomes culturally sustaining—institutionalized as the pedagogical norm, thereby "sustaining cultural and linguistic strengths in the lives of students and society."

Distinguishing this book from other texts focusing on culturally relevant teaching, this volume offers several distinctive features. It focuses not only on classroom practices but on (a) the highs, lows, and negotiations necessary to create effective university–school partnerships; and (b) ways that reflections on culturally relevant practices can influence the move toward sustaining humanizing and decolonizing practices in the lives and communities of students and teachers. In a world that is far from post-colonial as its institutions continue to be dominated by colonial European thought, the book provides background, motivation, and specific classroom examples for teachers, administrators, and teacher educators willing to change the long-held status quo.

Like the other books in our NCTE-Routledge Research Series, this book takes a critical look at classroom literacy practices and the ways in which literacy research and practice must attend to the lives of people of Color within and beyond P–12 literacy classrooms. The scope of books in our series includes an explicit focus on equity, justice, and antiracist literacy education; critical qualitative, quantitative, and mixed methodologies; a range of cutting-edge perspectives and approaches (e.g., sociocultural, cognitive, feminist, linguistic, pedagogical, critical, historical, anthropological); and research on the literacies of minoritized peoples as well as on diverse contexts (e.g., classrooms, school systems, families, communities) and forms of literacy (e.g., print, electronic, popular media).

We hope you are moved to action in your own educational settings by the stories of challenge, persistence, and attention to the literate lives of young children told in this book. Nash, Glover, and Polson's text joins other books in our series that have been carefully selected for their commitment to the role of educators in moving us toward a more equitable society.

Valerie Kinloch
Renée and Richard Goldman Dean and Professor of Education
University of Pittsburgh
USA

and

Susi Long
Professor, Instruction and Teacher Education
University of South Carolina, Columbia
USA

FOREWORD

"Are there any books focused on culturally sustaining pedagogy with young children?" "Where are the research and practice-based examples of educators sustaining the valued languages, literacies, and lifeways of very young learners of Color?" These are two versions of a question I often get when working with educators on how to enact culturally sustaining pedagogy (CSP). Reading through and learning with this necessary volume of nuanced examples of CSP in the early literacy classroom gave me so much joy: Finally, I have a powerful book to recommend! Simply put, this book will be treasured by early childhood educators, teacher educators, and all of us who are committed to sustaining the youngest in our communities across their educations and far beyond.

I have to admit I was a bit nervous about agreeing to write this foreword. I was fortunate to spend time learning with the authors in this volume some years ago during a National Council of Teachers of English (NCTE) Annual Convention session. They had invited me to be a discussant given their important work together enacting *culturally relevant pedagogy* (CRP) (Ladson-Billings, 1995) and their recent reading of my then early work on CSP. I learned much in that session, including how rightly anchored their (all three of them!) work was in the tenets of CRP. In agreeing to write this foreword I was nervous that CSP might not be central to the work (believe me, there is much work that says it is CRP *and* CSP without being either!). And let me say that work anchored solely in CRP has been and continues to be needed and powerful. But if I'm going to write about CSP, the work has to take up CSP. As I opened these pages I was hopeful the authors would take up CSP in generative and critical ways, while also understanding CSP's foundational relationship to CRP as the place where the "beat drops" (Ladson-Billings, 2014). I was so happy to see this is exactly what this needed group of deeply researched, felt, and relational chapters does.

So let me begin there: This book is importantly anchored in CRP but also seeks to (and does!) offer evidence of CSP. Indeed, one major contribution of the work is the ways in which the six chapters embody the ways CRP remains essential in our collective work as we push toward an education that *sustains* young people, their valued lifeways, and their communities through our teaching and learning. The chapters show how we can remain true to needed theoretical anchors while deepening and extending our work as new research, theories, and experiences enter our teaching practice.

Another way this book immediately drew me in was the ways the authors are very direct about Indigenous, Black, and Latinx theories and knowledges being at the foundation of their enactments of CSP. This is vital as CSP has always been a project grounded in solidarities and coalitions between Native, Black, Latinx, as well as Asian and Pacific Islander communities. In particular, CSP as an approach and an ongoing education movement understands the foundational settler colonial relationships between land theft, genocide, and enslavement and their ongoing legacies across U.S. nation-state institutions, including our schools. And, of course, CSP understands the always and ongoing projects of Native, Black, and Brown resistance, liberation, and love as the foundation for education settings that have always sustained our young people and communities. Indeed, the ways this book historicizes these connections in theory *and* practice are necessary to any project that calls itself CSP. This is crucial as CSP is a name for something our communities have always done through teaching and learning, even as nation-state schools have often played the opposite role. What makes this book so important is that it shows the ways teachers and teacher educators continue to reclaim and reimagine schools as sites for powerful enactments of CRP and CSP.

Central to CSP as a project of solidarity and coalition has been that our writing, research, and teaching has always centered Native, Black, Latinx, Asian, Pacific Islander educators working with students, families, and settings sustaining young people in their communities. As well, there have been some critical White educators in solidarity with communities in our broader CSP project. This book's necessary grounding in enactments of CRP and CSP implemented by teachers and teacher educators of Color with students and communities of Color is a deep CSP commitment, one that we know the profession needs because it is what our young people need. This commitment is lived in this book through the NCTE-supported professional dyad structure of teacher educators of Color (and one critical White teacher educator) learning in collaboration with teachers of Color. Inspired by the NCTE Cultivating New Voices among Scholars of Color (CNV) program, these dyads offer us a model of critical, sustaining partnerships. And they remind us that we cannot (and our communities never could) do the work of CSP alone. CSP is a collective project and any attempts to grow this work through teacher education and professional development will learn much from this book about the central role of partnership between teachers, school leaders, and teacher educators of Color.

Taking up five central features of culturally sustaining settings (critical centering, community accountability, historicizing, contending with internalized oppressions, the ability to curricularize), these chapters offer portraits of what CSP looks like across pre-school and the early grades. I was so thankful to see these features seriously engaged as they have been consistent across the CSP settings we have studied and contributed to. One of most important parts of the book is that the authors don't shy away from the very real tensions in enacting these features in a schooling system designed in opposition to each of them. School policies and, too often, our colleagues in classrooms (from pre-schools to universities) are set on upholding the status quo. CSP is resistance work and these chapters show us what that resistance looks and feels like for teachers, teacher educators, young people, and families. This last point about families is crucial. More and more we have understood CSP as necessarily intergenerational: The chapters in this book show how the very young can and must collaborate with educators and community members across generations in sustaining their language, literacies, and lives through education. Even as schools are designed to have one adult educator teaching a large group of young people, CSP requires we re-design (and reclaim) for intergenerationality.

A few months ago, frustrated with reading and seeing folks using what they called CSP merely for more access to the status quo, I tweeted:

> To be clear, the goal of culturally sustaining pedagogy is NOT more access to the same racist settler cis-hetero patriarchal ableist capitalist society. It is to revitalize & transform society through critically sustaining Native, Black, Latinx, Asian, Pacific Islander lifeways

The transformative educators who authored this book understand this and push in small and sometime big ways to show how it can and must happen with the youngest ones among us. CSP is about revitalizing and transforming, about ultimately undoing schooling as we know it to return to and imagine anew the ways our communities have sustained and must sustain each other, our society, our planet. As we continue to build together, I remain grateful for projects like this book, which are part of our collective effort to sustain the world we need, with our ancestors, our young ones, our elders, forward...

Django Paris
James A. and Cherry A. Banks Professor
of Multicultural Education
University of Washington
USA

ACKNOWLEDGEMENTS

First and foremost, we are endlessly grateful for Susi Long, whose peerless and tireless editing made this book what it is, and did not let it become something it was not meant to be. We also acknowledge the thoughtful suggestions of Valerie Kinloch, whose encouragement and words of wisdom have always served to lift us up as we worked to bring this book to fruition.

Many thanks are also due to Django Paris, whose collaborative thinking on culturally sustaining pedagogies has deeply inspired all three of us. We are thankful he saw the potential of moving toward culturally sustaining pedagogies in early childhood contexts, and feel truly honored that he has written the foreword to this book. Many thanks are due to Karen Adler and her team for their encouragement and careful editing.

Finally, we acknowledge the Professional Dyads in Culturally Relevant Teaching (PDCRT) and the National Council of Teachers of English (NCTE). The PDCRT's model of university–teacher collaboration around culturally relevant teaching enabled the learning featured in this book and continues to foster long-lasting partnerships and accessible scholarship on culturally relevant teaching in early childhood contexts.

We are eternally grateful for our families and friends-who-are-family, whose love, encouragement, and patience helped us see this book through to the end. We thank Carolyn Owerka for sheltering us in her Central Harlem brownstone while we put the finishing touches on the book. Below, we each offer acknowledgements to those helped us through the publication of this text, and who continue to shape who we are today.

Kindel

To Malik Nash and all of our Nashlings—Anisa, Taja, Salim, and Karim—a million thank yous for your bottomless patience and encouragement. To my parents, Earl Turner, Lloyce Nelson, and Allison Tillinghast, and to my academic mothers, Gloria Boutte, Etta Hollins, and Susi Long—without your collective mentorship and encouragement, I would be nowhere close to where I am today. To my sisters Fatima Rhett, Sarah Tillinghast, Mary Stevens, and Elena Hampton-Stover; and my sisterscholars Joy Howard, Candace Thompson, Timberly Baker, Katya Strekalova-Hughes, and Keisha Allen—as the African proverb goes, I am because we are.

Crystal

To the love of my life, Chioke—I am amazed by your selfless support and fueled by your endless encouragement. Thank you for sharing in my success and lifting me up when I needed a boost. Ma—Thank you for showing me the meaning of unconditional love. You will always be my rock, my biggest cheerleader, and the wind beneath my wings. Dad—You never doubt my potential. I am inspired by your faith and humbled by your love. To Granny, Mama, Daddy, Auntie Sister, and Di—I hope I made you proud!

Bilal

To the loving memory of my dad, Hugh Polson, my mother-in-law, Lidia Moyano, my very first dance teacher, Mary A. Baird, and my god-parents, Bilal and Rahkiah Abdurahim. I am grateful for the love and grace of my wife, Patty, and the power and energy of our sons, Aliasha and Malachi. Thank you to my mommy and mother, Florence Polson. Finally, I'd like to give a special shout out to the families, students, and loving school family of the great Northern Parkway School.

References

Ladson-Billings, G. (1995). Toward a theory of culturally relevant pedagogy. *American Educational Research Journal*, 32, 465–491.

Ladson-Billings, G. (2014). Culturally relevant pedagogy 2.0: a.k.a. the remix. *Harvard Educational Review*, 84, 74–84.

1

EDUCATION FOR THE HUMAN SOUL

Culturally Sustaining Pedagogies and the Legacy of Love That Guides Us

Kindel Nash, Bilal Polson, and Crystal Glover

> Education for the human soul … give[s] power and the right direction to the intellect, the sensibilities, and the will.
>
> –*Anna Julia Cooper (1892)*

Django Paris and Samy Alim (2014) said, in a groundbreaking reflection on culturally sustaining pedagogies:

> We move away from the pervasiveness of pedagogies that are too closely aligned with linguistic, literate, and cultural hegemony and toward developing a pedagogical agenda that does not concern itself with the seemingly panoptic 'White gaze' (Morrison, 1998) that permeates educational research and practice with and for students of color, their teachers, and their schools. (Paris & Alim, 2014, p. 86)

Their words and those of educator-activist Anna Julia Cooper (1892) as change agents more than a century apart from each other indicate that the urgent need for justice in educational spaces has not yet been successfully addressed. Charging us to engage in transformational love and education for the human soul, these educators play a strong role in framing the moral, philosophical, methodological, and pedagogical convictions that guide this volume. This book shares the stories of early literacy teachers and teacher educators who honor children and their families and communities and recognize the urgent need for pedagogical change. Guided by educators like Anna Julia Cooper, we focused on *education for the human soul* as we set out to develop culturally relevant practices in our classrooms and, through the writing of this book, began to ask questions posed by Paris and Alim (2017a, n.p.): How can our pedagogies be culturally sustaining and what is it we seek to sustain?

Foundationally, the educators in this book built their teaching on the tenets of culturally relevant pedagogy (CRP). As conceptualized by Gloria Ladson-Billings (1995), CRP has three goals: building students' cultural competence, critical consciousness, and academic achievement. The concept of culturally sustaining pedagogies (CSP) (detailed later in this chapter) came into our worlds when we read the work of Django Paris (2012), who suggested it as an expansion and loving critique of Ladson-Billings' (1995, 2009, 2014) ideas. Paris built on the legacy of CRP by focusing on ways CSP can contribute to the ongoing work of educational justice that CRP and other asset pedagogies have advanced (Paris, 2014), while emphasizing heritage and community practices as dynamic, not static, and insisting on pedagogies that sustain "linguistically and culturally dexterous ways of being" (Paris & Alim, 2014, p. 91). Thus, while much of Paris and Alim's articulation of culturally sustaining pedagogy honors Ladson-Billings' intent by centering community languages, practices, and knowledge; ensuring student agency and community input; and developing students' capacity to address oppression, their move to *sustain* requires particular attention to maintaining "linguistic, literate, and cultural pluralism as a part of the democratic project of schooling" (Paris, 2013, p. 95). This, in our view, means affecting institutional as well as day-to-day changes in individual classrooms so that cultural relevance, linguistic and cultural pluralism become normalized, embraced, and centered in the institutions of schooling, the lives of students, families, and the broader society. We understand this to mean a rejection of the dominance of the White gaze (Morrison, 1998) or, as Alim and Paris (2017) put it,

> liberating ourselves from this gaze … [moving] away from the White imperialist project [to engage in the] "collective struggle against an educational system that contains us and toward one that sustains us … [shifting] the discourse about who we think the mainstream is not just because of demographic change but because [we] see inequality." (Alim & Paris, 2017, pp. 13–15)

CRP (as the ideology that prompted our initial work) and CSP (as the philosophy that we strive to understand and embody) play key roles in the stories told by four teacher–teacher educator pairs/partners (dyads) in this book. These educators worked together for two years in richly diverse, multilingual classrooms across the United States through a project called Professional Dyads and Culturally Relevant Teaching (PDCRT), funded by the National Council of Teachers of English (NCTE). PDCRT was initially inspired by another NCTE initiative, Cultivating New Voices Among Scholars of Color (CNV) (Kinloch, 2011), which was developed by Arnetha Ball, Carol Lee, and Peter Smagorinsky and directed at different times through the last 20 years by Peter Smagorinsky, Maria Franquiz, Valerie Kinloch, and Juan Guerra. CNV pairs experienced scholars (Mentors) with doctoral students or early-career scholars of Color (Fellows) to support and foreground critical research in literacy education. With this impetus and inspiration, Susi Long and Erin Miller initiated the idea for PDCRT also drawing from Susi's work with Carmen Tisdale and Janice Baines (Baines, Tisdale, & Long, 2018). It was envisioned as a program that would pair classroom teachers and teacher educators (dyads) as mutual mentors learning from and with each other as they generated culturally relevant practices in early childhood classrooms. Joined by Mariana Souto-Manning and Dinah Volk as an initial planning and leadership team, the idea was refined and proposed to NCTE's Executive Committee in 2012. Established officially in 2013, the first two-year cohort of PDCRT dyads was funded by NCTE's Executive Committee as a pilot project. As this book goes to press, PDCRT is welcoming its fourth cohort of dyads. This book represents the work of four dyads from the charter PDCRT cohort (2013–2015).

PDCRT's purpose as outlined in the original proposal was to

> create a space within NCTE for supporting early childhood Educators of Color and educators who teach children of color, English Language Learners, and children from low-income communities in: (1) generating, implementing, documenting, evaluating, and disseminating culturally relevant pedagogies in early childhood literacy; and (2) becoming more involved in NCTE, eventually in governance structures. (2013)

The project focuses on fostering and researching culturally relevant teaching as fruitful pedagogies deeply connected to centering languages, ethnicities, identities that have been erased or ignored in society and schooling. It focuses on six goals introduced here (Figure 1.1) but expanded upon from the perspective of many of the PDCRT's founders in Chapter Six.

Across university–school and geographic contexts, PDCRT dyads research, generate, implement, document, and evaluate culturally relevant literacy practices in early childhood classrooms. As explored in this book, we have come to see many of those practices as critical elements in not only culturally relevant but also culturally sustaining work. This chapter introduces readers to our work. Through it we describe the book's contents and organization, the theoretical ideas and sociopolitical convictions that guide us, and the humanizing approach that teachers in this book

1. Develop culturally relevant pedagogies in early childhood (PreK–Grade 3) classrooms
2. Create mutual mentorships and dismantle university–school hierarchies
3. Provide a support system for getting started with culturally relevant teaching
4. Prioritize diverse classrooms and teachers of Color, cultivating their professional leadership
5. Transform early childhood spaces into places for critical conversations

FIGURE 1.1 Professional Dyads in Culturally Relevant Teaching (PDCRT) goals.

took toward developing practices and documenting and analyzing their work with children and families. Finally, this chapter raises the question about what it will take for this work to be sustained in the efforts to:

> Combat and eradicate oppressive, racist, educational policies that advantage monoculturalism, that debase the linguistic virtuosities of communities of color, and that recode terms such as relevance and responsiveness to mark tolerance over acceptance, normalization over difference, demonization over humanization, and hate over love. (Kinloch, 2017, p. 29)

This Book

The words in the subtitle of this book, "Honoring Children," comes from a conversation that took place a couple of years ago among members of the charter PDCRT cohort when we met at the NCTE Annual Convention. In discussing the theoretical framework that would anchor this book, each of us shared our thoughts about what the work, at its core, was about. At one point, teacher and Chapter Four co-author Alicia Arce-Boardman said that, for her, "this work is about honoring children." Everyone around the table knew that she had captured the essence of our work. When we say those words, however, it is important to know that we are not merely promoting a funds of knowledge approach, nor are we merely acknowledging that children bring multiple rich and legitimate languages, histories, and identities to the classroom. For us, *honoring children* carries important responsibilities to alter the Eurocratic status quo (King & Swartz, 2018) in schools and to re-center and pedagogically normalize languages, cultures, heritages, and ways of being that have been oppressed through systems that define what counts in schooling and society.

With that foundation in mind, this book shares examples from the classroom experiences of four dyads, contributing to bodies of work that address the following issues: (a) the absence of culturally relevant practices as sustained and systemic in early childhood classrooms in spite of volumes of work suggesting that such teaching is essential to teaching all students (Au, 1979; Gay, 2010; Genishi & Dyson, 2009; Hollins, 2015; Paris & Alim, 2017b; Woodson, 1933); (b) schools' continued lack of success in educating young children of Color, emergent bi/multilingual children, and children from low-income households, to the same levels of literacy proficiency as that of their White,[1] middle-class, English-only peers (National Center for Education Statistics [NCES], 2016); and (c) limited understandings about the impact of university–school partnerships working/researching together as mutual learning partners in classrooms and with children and families.

The need for potent examples of early childhood literacy teaching and assessment that counter the narrowly conceived norm is great. As Long (2011) offered, "without examples of inspirational teaching … too many teachers will not realize the tremendous agency (voice and choice) they have, and they will continue to feel constrained" (p. vii). Sharing new approaches, strategies, and practices, we fulfill a prominent need for early childhood teachers to develop pedagogies that might be sustained based on remixing and recentering the cultures of children (Ladson-Billings, 2017) and the development of children's critical consciousness within a "deep knowledge of the particular context in which schools are located" (Hollins, 2015, p. 2).

The dyads who are chapter authors in this book are all teachers and teacher educators of Color except one teacher educator, committed to antiracist practices, who worked in classrooms that predominantly served children of Color. Thus, this volume shares examples and practices predominantly from *teachers of Color* and *their students of Color*. This is significant, for while scholars have argued for decades about the significance of forefronting the work of teachers of Color (Foster, 1997; Irvine, 2003; Milner, 2008), with the exception of *Reading, Writing, and Talk* (2017) by Mariana Souto-Manning and Jessica Martell and *We've Been Doing it Your Way Long Enough: Choosing the Culturally Relevant Classroom* (2018) by Janice Baines, Carmen Tisdale, and Susi Long, few early childhood literacy texts center on the practices of teachers and children of Color authored by educators of Color.

Throughout this book are examples of practices such as translanguaging, warm demanding teaching; a Latina mothers' support group; selecting and creating culturally sustaining books; and valuing and organizing children's study of their histories, languages, and cultures along with revered figures in sports, popular culture, music, and literacies. These and other practices featured in the chapters of this volume critically center on community languages and literacies and honor family and community ways of knowing. Importantly, these practices, which extend from and are accountable to children, families, and their communities, establish *confianza* and use multiple means to communicate with families, and employ authentic, contextualized, translanguaged assessments. In this way, the book offers examples of historicized practices that try to disrupt the colonized histories of communities, showcasing opportunities for children and families to confront oppressive and colonizing messages by acting on issues of racism, immigration, fairness, and justice.

The definitive goals of culturally relevant teaching are to build students' cultural competence and sociopolitical consciousness, and increase student achievement (Ladson-Billings, 1995, 2014) while critiquing the norms that delimit what counts as achievement (Kinloch, 2017). Demonstrating how children can grow academically when their languages, literacies, cultures, and histories are centered rather than denied, degraded, or moved to the margins (Alim & Paris, 2017), we provide qualitative and quantitative data to show connections among these pedagogies and children's motivation, engagement, achievement, and proficiency in literacy.

In these pages, we also focus on the *processes* that the teacher–teacher educator dyads experienced as they worked to develop authentic and critically collaborative, mutual mentoring relationships within the teacher–teacher educator partnership. As such, we offer practical strategies for teachers, teacher educators, and others to work together to generate and implement culturally relevant early literacy pedagogies and work toward their sustainability in students' lives as well as normalized within partnerships centered around co-research, collaboration, and advocacy. It is the sustainability that we bring to the forefront in this work, recognizing that acknowledging relevance is a first step but without sustainability, these practices become merely the work of one teacher in one moment in time. Thus, a pedagogical journey which began with a commitment to generating, documenting, evaluating, and disseminating culturally relevant pedagogies that engaged teacher educators and teachers learning together, has grown through the writing of this book and the inspiration of Paris and Alim to ask: How can this work and the cultural ways of being of communities of Color be sustained in the lives of the children and their communities and normalized in educational institutions?

Theoretical Framework: The Family Tree That Guides Us

Gloria Ladson-Billings (1995) entreated teachers long ago to anchor their instruction in what she called culturally relevant teaching. She offered that great teaching should be asset based, but going further than that, it should develop students' (a) competence in their own and at least one other culture; (b) critical consciousness regarding injustices; and (c) academic achievement. In 2014, admiring Paris's conceptualization of culturally sustaining pedagogy "as the place where the [culturally relevant] 'beat drops'" (p. 76), Ladson-Billings (2014) wrote about culturally sustaining pedagogy as an important outgrowth of culturally relevant teaching. We believe that both concepts are critically important. As Baines (Baines et al., 2018) reminded us, "no other approach is viable without appreciating relevance … if we do not see relevance in the lives and histories that are most marginalized … we will not have the foundation needed to liberate, emancipate, or sustain relevance" (p. 12). Thus, in this book, authors write primarily about culturally relevant pedagogies (Ladson-Billings, 1995) with some referencing culturally responsive teaching (Gay, 2010), but we are also committed to sustaining students' cultural and linguistic ways of knowing in their lives and in educational institutions "as part of schooling for positive social transformation and revitalization" (Paris & Alim, 2014, p. 88). Our interest in expanding our work to understand and embrace culturally sustaining pedagogy comes from our dedication to normalizing rather than eradicating the cultural ways of being of communities of Color as we seek to:

> Foster—to sustain—linguistic, literate, and cultural pluralism as part of schooling for positive social transformation and revitalization [positioning] cultural dexterity as a necessary good, and sees the outcome of learning as additive, rather than subtractive, as remaining whole rather than framed as

> broken, as critically enriching strengths rather than replacing deficits … existing wherever the lifeways of communities who have been and continue to be damaged and erased through schooling … [calling for] schooling to be a site for sustaining—rather than eradicating—the cultural ways of being of communities of color. (Paris & Alim, 2014, p. 88)

This commitment builds directly on the work of generations of educator-scholars whose legacy informs this book's theoretical framework. We describe our theoretical framework using the metaphor of a family tree (Figure 1.2), invoked to communicate the history, lineage, heritage, and legacies on which the dyad work was built, ultimately leading to our convictions about culturally relevant and later sustaining pedagogies. Our family tree signifies that, for more than a century, Black, Latinx, and Indigenous thought pioneers have contributed to a rich expanse of literature urging us to develop educational programs, policies, and practices to create an equitable society and equitable schools. Our family tree also recognizes that the legal reforms and social movements that have historically informed change in schools have done so in response to the sociopolitical context of the United States, where the "languages, literacies, histories, and cultural ways of being" of communities of Color are prevalently viewed as "pathological" (Alim & Paris, 2017, p. 2). Through deliberately connecting the progenitors of Black, Latinx, and Indigenous intellectual scholarship to critical theories/theorists and culturally sustaining pedagogies and its theoretical precursors, we strive for a remembering of worldviews often omitted or distorted in theories and scholarship of early childhood teaching (Boutte, 2015; King & Swartz, 2015).

In the following sections, we describe our philosophical and theoretical **roots,** Black, Latinx, and Indigenous/Native radical intellectual thought and critical pedagogies; **trunk,** legal reforms and sociopolitical movements; **branches,** asset-based theories and pedagogies; and **leaves and fruits,** culturally relevant, responsive, and sustaining pedagogies. We find leaves and fruit fitting metaphors for the way heritage and community-based, culturally relevant, responsive, and sustaining pedagogies directly link to a lineage of asset-based pedagogies, legal reforms, and sociopolitical movements, and a multifaceted root system of Black, Latinx, and Indigenous scholarship and pedagogies. These tree-based metaphors allow us to situate PDCRT's collaborative work with young children, families, communities, and colleagues within an extended, deeply rooted network and history of scholarship and leadership. The educators and activists we honor through this family tree represent a rich history of work dedicated to providing and promoting equitable education to children who have been discriminated against and marginalized. These are scholars, activists, and movements valued by us personally and reflective of our thinking at this moment in time.

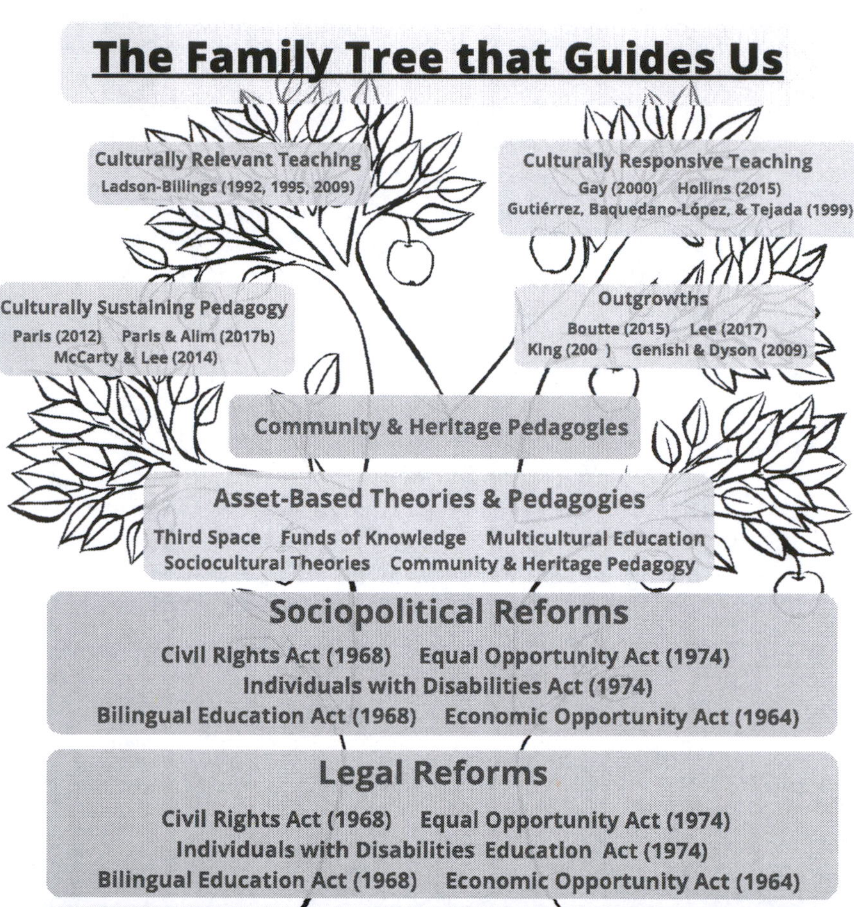

FIGURE 1.2 The family tree that guides us.

The Roots

The roots of our family tree acknowledge scholars who, for us, represent a foundational lineage connecting to culturally relevant, responsive, and sustaining pedagogies. We believe Black, Latinx, and Indigenous scholars from the late nineteenth and early twentieth centuries have constantly and powerfully shaped the arc of pedagogies that are culturally grounded and, at times, anti-colonial. By also representing critical pedagogies at the roots of our family tree, we acknowledge the ways in which these and other scholars influenced *pedagogies* which attend to the roots of colonialism and oppression "as both an ongoing and incomplete project, with internal contradictions, cracks, and fissures" (McCoy, Tuck, & McKenzie, 2016, p. 8). Critical pedagogies are crucial, since schools have long served as the setting whereby students are enculturated to a rightness of European norms (Lomawaima & McCarty, 2006; Long, Souto-Manning, & Vasquez, 2016; through the transmission and production of White practices and ways of being (Miller, 2015). Unearthing these roots, we glean wisdom that informs our thinking about early childhood classrooms and schools as crucial sites of advocacy for freedom and legitimization of the continued struggles of all marginalized people.

Black[2] Radical Intellectual Thought

Grant, Brown, and Brown (2016) remind us that the life projects of many radical Black thinkers "are victims of historical distortion, omission, and inaccuracies in US textbooks and other places where historical information is shared" (p. vii). Although often omitted and distorted in history, centuries of African innovations, whether scientific, philosophical, mathematical, artistic, literary, or otherwise, have been delineated in research and scholarship, showing the influence of African thinking on the Greeks and Romans (see Appiah & Gates, 2005; Diop, 1991). We draw wisdom from the many radical Black intellectuals and historians who were/are rooted in this African-centric knowledge, and who have advocated for those who have been dehumanized and degraded in American society and schools (see Martin Delany, 1812–1885; Chancellor Williams, 1883–1992; G. M. James, 1893–1956; John G. Jackson, 1907–1993; John Henrik Clark, 1915–1998; Yosef Ben-Jochannan, 1918–2015; Ivan Van Sertima, 1935–2009; Marian Wright Edelman, 1939–present; Asa Hilliard, 1933–2007; Molefi Asante, 1942–present; Arthur Schomburg, 1874–1938). We also recognize the direct links between their scholarship and the Black and Africana studies movements on university campuses that continue today.

We draw particular attention to the foundational but often neglected words and work of Sojourner Truth, Anna Julia Cooper, Carter G. Woodson, Martin Delany, and Alain Locke, as their thought work in the early eighteenth and nineteenth centuries connects, both to the individuals referenced above, and to culturally sustaining pedagogies today. We write briefly to honor these scholars here but detailed analyses about Anna Julia Cooper, Carter G. Woodson, and Alain Leroy Locke can be found in Grant, Brown, and Brown's (2016) volume *Black Intellectual Thought in Education: The Missing Traditions of Anna Julia Cooper, Carter G. Woodson, and Alain Leroy Locke* and the work of Sojourner Truth and Martin Delany (1879) can be found in multiple volumes, for example Painter (1996), Lee (2017), and Asante (2012).

Sojourner Truth's (1791–1883) experiences as an enslaved person led to her vow that she would overcome those who attempted to control her. Born Isabella Baumfree, she created a new identity with the name Sojourner Truth (Painter, 1996). We view Sojourner Truth's renaming, along with her activism for people of Color within 19th century suffragist and abolitionist movements as a fundamental assertion of her humanness. In other words, by shedding her European name and by speaking the truth through her activism for people of Color, she confronted and disrupted the atrocity of human enslavement. Her powerful assertion of humanity is foundationally connected to culturally sustaining pedagogies' disruption of the ideology that marginalizes people's identities as *other than*, while "White and middle or upper-class [people] are just human" (Lee, 2017, pp. 262–263).

Martin Delany's (1812–1885) philosophy and activism catalyzed what is now known as Afrocentric or African-centric thought. A freeborn abolitionist, journalist, and researcher, Delany studied medicine at Harvard University and culture in Western Africa. Delany was the first African American field officer in the United States Army during the Civil War. Martin Delany's ideas promoted racial pride and self-help, advocating for African American immigration to central South America, the Caribbean, and Africa. Delany's work as publisher, world explorer, and entrepreneur reestablished connections between African American and African history (Asante, 2012; Behnken, Smithers, & Wendt, 2017).

Anna Julia Cooper (1858–1964), a scholar, teacher, activist, and school administrator, advocated, like Sojourner Truth, for the rights of women of Color (Lemert & Bhan, 1998). Her experiences as a formerly enslaved person who progressed to be the recipient of multiple graduate degrees, and as the only Black woman lecturer at the Pan-African Congress in London in 1900 and the World's Congress of Representative Women in 1903, contributed to her humanizing vision of education. Her legacy endures today in the justice pedagogies of educators who seek to sustain communities (Cooper, 1892; Grant et al., 2016).

Carter G. Woodson's (1875–1950) explicit focus on curriculum reform in and for Black public schools (Grant et al., 2016) deeply informs and links with our move toward community and heritage pedagogies that are culturally sustaining. Like educators who strive to enact pedagogies that are culturally relevant, responsive, and sustaining, Woodson believed that education which espoused White supremacy by focusing primarily on European contributions, texts, ideologies, and histories failed to recognize the contributions of African Americans (Woodson, 1933).

Alain Locke (1885–1954), an African American philosopher and educator and member of the Bahá'í faith, is widely known as the "Father of the Harlem Renaissance." Unlike other Black leaders of the time, such as Woodson and W. E. B. DuBois, Locke endorsed the importance of self-promotion, aligning with culturally sustaining pedagogies' goal to "challenge and change the system of oppression in which [pedagogies] are embedded" (Irizarry, 2017, p. 83). The critical and radical ideologies of Black empowerment engendered by Truth, Cooper, Woodson, and Locke, among so many others, created fertile ground for the growth of sociopolitical movements, legal actions, and scholarship that fostered asset-based pedagogies.

Latinx[3] Radical Intellectual Thought

With culturally sustaining pedagogies' goal of combatting "oppressive educational and social policies" (Paris & Alim, 2014, p. 89), understanding the deep roots of Latinx intellectual history, thought, and resistance in this country is also particularly important to consider as:

> The oppression and exploitation of Latinos (like Asians) have historical roots unknown to most Americans. People who learn at least a little about Black [people] remain totally ignorant about how the United States seized half of Mexico or how it colonized Puerto Rico. (Martínez, 2000, p. 97)

We share information about Latinx leaders who have inspired us through their heroic efforts long ago that connect deeply to culturally sustaining pedagogies' present goal to sustain language and culture as "crucial form[s] of sustenance in its own right" (Bucholtz, Casillas, & Lee, 2017, p. 44). Antonia Pantoja, Luisa Capetillo, Genera Pagán, Pedro Albizu Campos (El Maestro), as well as members of the Idar family and movements/organizations like Aspira, El Primer Congreso Mexicanista, and the League of United Latin American Citizens (LULAC), fought to preserve Latinx language, culture, race, and basic human rights in schools during the late nineteenth and early twentieth centuries and their legacies inspire our work today.

Antonia Pantoja (1922–2002) was a charismatic social worker, professor, community activist, and founder of the instrumental organization Aspira, which promoted equitable education, leadership, and organization for Puerto Ricans on the U.S. mainland (Nuñez, 2009). Under Pantoja's leadership, Aspira was instrumental in organizing and ultimately helping pass legislation mandating bilingual education in public schools (Nuñez, 2009).

Luisa Capetillo (1879–1922) was a union leader, writer, and journalist in Puerto Rico. She published several books reflecting on the agency of Latinx women and the importance of working towards a society free of oppressive structures (Torres & Vásquez 2003, p. 178). Like Capetillo, Genera Pagán (1897–1963) worked in tobacco factories and fought for women's rights in Puerto Rico. After passage of the Nineteenth Amendment, which granted White women (not women of Color) the right to vote, Pagán continued to fight for the rights of Puerto Rican women (Torres & Vásquez, 2003, p. 180). Luisa Capetillo, Antonia Pantoja, and Genera Pagán worked to forefront the strengths of Latinx communities and languages, while fighting against oppressive structural barriers during their time. In the same way, educators engaged in culturally sustaining pedagogies today strive to "maintain the longstanding cultural practices of communities of color while ... also learn[ing] to critique dominant power structures" (Alim & Paris, 2017, p. 2).

Pedro Albizu Campos (1891–1965) also played a major role in the struggle for Puerto Rican independence from American colonial oppression. His activism and ideology "promoted national symbols and observances that kept alive independentista sentiment in Puerto Rico's cultural and political life" (Meyer, 2011, p. 89). Members of the Idar family, prominent journalists from Laredo, Texas lead by Nicasio Idar (father, b. 1853), a journalist and printer, published an independent newspaper, *La Crónica*, that took on racism and linguicism in public schools (Torres & Vásquez, 2003, pp. 222–223). Their fight eventually led to a regional convention, El Primer Congreso Mexicanista (1911), which, through court challenges, began to work toward changing unjust school policies targeting Latinx and Chicano Americans.

LULAC, a national, non-political organization formed during the 1920s and 1930s, focused on creating a space for Latinx people to express and fight for their rights as United States citizens. Like the Congreso Mexicanista, LULAC—still the largest, oldest Latinx civil rights group in the country—joined legal challenges to fight unjust school policies like English-only, segregated schools (Navarro & Mejia, 2004). Comparable to the work of the Black thinkers described previously, Pantoja, Campos, Capetillo, Pagán, the Idar family, and LULAC created sustaining spaces that accounted for the lived experiences of their people. Their struggles inform our work as they provide robust historical examples of people of Color "sustaining minds and bodies within a system that often has the exact opposite goals" (Alim & Paris, 2017, p. 13).

Indigenous Radical Intellectual Thought

The experiences of Indigenous peoples in this country intersect with those of other minoritized groups. Here we recognize untold histories and confront stereotypical and distorted narratives about Indigenous people that seem deeply ingrained in the American mind. As Vine Deloria (1969) wrote:

> The American public feels most comfortable with the mythical Indians of stereotype-land who were always THERE. These Indians are fierce, they wear feathers and grunt. Most of us don't fit this idealized figure since we grunt only when overeating, which is seldom. To be an Indian in modern American society is in a very real sense to be unreal and ahistorical. (p. 2)

Like Black and Latinx history in this country, Indigenous American history does not begin with enslavement, subjugation, and oppression through American legal policies such as the Bureau of Indian Affairs Indian Boarding Schools, which systematically sought to "erase languages, parenting practices, and belief systems and replace them with European models" (Long et al., 2016, p. 14). Indigenous America is rooted in a fertile history, originating long before European colonists. Honoring those histories, we offer the perspectives of some of the forerunners of thinking, movements, and events that fostered culturally based pedagogies in Indigenous communities; the Ghost Dance Movement, the Massacre at Wounded Knee, and the intellectual legacies of Black Elk, Chief Sitting Bull, and Luther Standing Bear.

For Indigenous peoples, "organized nationalist, non-cooperationist political resistance came primarily in the form of religious movements that did not produce books, publish newspapers, or … [form] national organizations" (Warrior, 1995, p. 11). Scholars of Indigenous thought cite two important, connected examples of such political resistance in the late nineteenth/early twentieth centuries, the Ghost Dance movement and the Wounded Knee Massacre. The Ghost Dance movement provided Indigenous Americans who had historically been brutally victimized by the government a glimpse of hope (Warrior, 1995). It originated in 1889 with the vision of a Paiute Indian chief, Wovoka, who "promised an end to Euro-American oppression and a return to tribal autonomy, abundance and spiritual renewal … deliverance required participation in a regime of ritual dance and prayer" (King, 2016, n.p.). What started as a peaceful religious movement ended in brutality and violence (Ostler, 2004), known as the Massacre at Wounded Knee. Black Elk (1863–1950), who would later reflect on the hope spurred by the Ghost Dance movement, was an Ogala Lakota holy man; one of the most studied Indigenous Americans of the late nineteenth/early twentieth centuries (Ostler, 2004). In an account of his childhood, Black Elk said, "But the Wasichus [White people] came, and they have made little islands … and always these islands are becoming smaller, for around them surges the gnawing flood of the Wasichu; and it is dirty with lies and greed" (Black Elk in Neihardt, 2014, p. 47).

Another important figure in Indigenous intellectual thinking, Luther Standing Bear (1868–1939), was born in the Dakota plains. We end this section with Standing Bear's words, as he questions us to think:

> Why not a school of Indian thought, built on the Indian pattern and conducted by Indian instructors? Why not a school of tribal art? Why should not America be cognizant of itself; aware of its identity? In short, why should not America be preserved? … In denying the Indian his ancestral rights and heritages the white race is but robbing itself. But America can be revived, rejuvenated, by recognizing a native school of thought. (Standing Bear, 1931/1988, pp. 254–255)

Black, Latinx, and Indigenous radical thinking and advocacy exemplify how the U.S. identity/motto of *e puburis unum* (out of many, one) has been created against a backdrop of resistance to violence and oppression. While these bodies of thought and associated movements led to institutional change, such as ethnic studies programs on many college campuses, violence and oppression persist, as members of #BlackLivesMatter, the National Network for Immigrant and Refugee Rights, and the Native Water Protectors at Standing Rock literally fight for sustenance of the bodies and minds of people of Color (Alim & Paris, 2017). The deep roots of radical Black, Latinx, and Indigenous American people, movements, and scholarship nurtured the growth of roots of critical pedagogical thought later in the twentieth century.

Critical Theories and Pedagogies

Critical theories, and their extending pedagogies, grew from the roots of Black, Latinx, and Indigenous scholar-activism. For example, Black and Latina feminisms in the poetic contributions of Audre Lorde, Gloria Anzaldúa, and Akasha Gloria Hull confront the same colonialism and oppression in the lived experiences of women of Color explored by Black, Latinx, and Indigenous scholar-activism from the previous century (Tuck & McKenzie, 2015). Similarly, Vine Deloria (1969), a prolific Indigenous scholar-activist, built on the legacy of the Ghost Dance movement to assert the need for both idealism and pragmatism in the continued struggle for Indigenous rights and freedoms. Likewise, Sandy Grande's (2004, 2015) *Red Pedagogy* elucidates how and why Indigenous theories of education, self-determination, and survival are intimately connected to past and present efforts to decolonize education. Although originating earlier, critical pedagogies experienced a collective insurgence during the 1960s and 1970s through the scholarship and activism of César Chávez, Gloria Anzaldúa, Audre Lorde, James Baldwin, Paulo Freire, Derrick Bell, Henry Giroux, Molefi Kete Asante, Akasha Gloria Hull, Betita Martínez, James Banks, Oscar Kawagley, Vine Deloria, K. Tsianina Lomawaima, Teresa McCarthy, Sande Grande, Ronald Takaki, Howard Zinn, and many others.

The goal of critical theories (and the pedagogies that extend from them) is to destabilize "master narratives and … dominant discourses" (Kincheloe, 2008, p. 125) about the world. Critical theorists, comprising radical feminists, critical legal scholars, critical race theorists, and African-centered and Black and Latina feminist thinkers have long reasoned against the dichotomous and colonizing superior/inferior system of morals, thoughts, and theories perpetuated in societies and institutions (Anzaldúa, 1999; Asante, 1992; Baldwin, 2013; Bell, 1992; DuBois, 1898/2001; hooks, 2014; Lorde, 2007).

In early childhood education, critical theory/pedagogies can be used as a *way of thinking* about how policies, stereotypes, dominant narratives, and practices influence the lives of the children we teach. Thus, critical theory/pedagogies can help us push the limits of education, as Freire (1993) said, "precisely because, in not being able to do everything, education can do something. As educators … it behooves us to see what we can do so that we can completely realize our goals" (p. 25). Since culturally sustaining pedagogies seek to "interrogate and critique the simultaneously progressive and oppressive currents," "contradictory forces," and "existing hegemonic discourses about … gender, race, sexuality, and citizenship" (Paris & Alim, 2014, p. 93), teachers who use these pedagogies need an understanding of the radical roots of critical theories and theorists. Further, radical, critical ideas and practices fueled legal reforms and sociopolitical movements. We describe these movements as the trunk of our metaphorical tree, honoring the family lineage of pedagogies that help us understand how to help all children navigate the complex terrain of schooling.

Trunk

Growing from the nutrients provided by a strong root system of Black, Latinx, and Native intellectual thought and critical pedagogies, the mid-twentieth century experienced abundant legal and sociopolitical reforms developed in response to the legal, social, political, and educational climate of the United States. The reforms of the 1960s and 1970s inexorably influenced the landscape of educational practices today (Banks & Banks, 2009), including culturally relevant, responsive, mediating, and sustaining pedagogies. We describe a few of the most significant reforms and movements here as actions that form the solid trunk of our framework.

Legal Reforms

The Economic Opportunity Act of 1964 led to the longstanding federal initiative of Head Start. Although not intended to forefront culturally relevant or culturally sustaining curricula, Head Start has fostered tremendous success in decreasing inequities in school achievement, high school graduation, and educational attainment for people of Color and other marginalized peoples (Johnson, Kalil, & Dunifon, 2010). The Civil Rights Act of 1968 led to forced busing to integrate schools, but was also highly problematic as students who had once excelled at schools such as those that Carter G. Woodson, and Anna Julia Cooper ran, suddenly found themselves in contexts that were disconnected from their socio-cultural-historical knowledge (Cole, 1995). The Bilingual Education Act of 1968 required schools to at least attend to the languages of students of Color and allowed funding to support educational programming for bi/multilingual students (Paris & Alim, 2014).

These three legislative acts contributed to the Individuals with Disabilities Education Act (1974), which fostered intellectual and educational reform and inquiry which has led to moves towards a core set of educational practices.

Augmenting these legislative actions, alliances between researchers and classroom teachers foregrounded research demonstrating that deficit approaches are not just (Ball, 1995; Paris & Alim, 2014; Souto-Manning & Martell, 2017). Taken together, legal actions and collaboration between teachers and scholars fostered an environment in which thinking about culturally relevant, responsive, mediating, and later sustaining pedagogies could grow.

Sociopolitical Movements

The Civil Rights Movement, the Black Power Movement, the Chicano/Latino Civil Rights Movement, and the Native Rights Movement connected to these legislative acts and their role as antecedents to thinking about culturally sustaining teaching. The Civil Rights Movement (1954–1968) resulted as "the courage of thousands of Black people and their white allies who refused to be intimidated by segregationist violence and disorder" (Bell, 2004, p. 8). It is possibly the most publicized collective effort on the part of Blacks and others to "demonstrate racial pride, orchestrate varying strategies of resistance, and to demand a connection to the social damages of enslavement, Jim and Jane Crow, and segregation" (Grant et al., 2016, pp. 6–7). The nonviolent protest and civil disobedience of this movement led to multiple federal-level court rulings (e.g., *Brown v. Board of Education I & II*) and subsequent policies facilitating some positive changes in White attitudes towards people of Color (Grant et al., 2016), mostly as a result of wide media coverage of White resistance to segregation that "appalled many who otherwise would have remained on the sidelines" (Bell, 2004, p. 7). Although it is by far the most intentionally distorted movement in the American psyche (see Theoharis, 2018), the justice-oriented work of the Civil Rights Movement persists today with the work of those who battle for equitable schools, colleges, healthcare, housing, and through teachers who enact pedagogies that are equitable and sustaining (Bonilla-Silva, 2006; Paris & Alim, 2014, 2017a).

Influenced by Malcolm X's teachings about self-determination and cultural pride (Joseph, 2006; Ongiri, 2009), the Black Power Movement commanded a deeper vision of democracy and "tested America's willingness to extend citizenship to blacks with a robust call for self-determination that scandalized and transformed long standing American institutions" (Joseph, 2006, p. 8). This movement directly connects to the pluralistic goal of culturally sustaining pedagogies, pushing back against "dominant narratives that superficially affirm differences and diversities while maintaining the status quo" (Kinloch, 2017, pp. 28–29). Like the Black Power Movement, culturally sustaining pedagogies resist "assimilationist and anti-democratic monolingual/monocultural educational policies" (Paris & Alim, 2014, p. 88).

The Chicano/Latino Civil Rights Movement of the 1960s and 1970s was a recuperation of Latinx thought and organization that, as you have seen, had taken root hundreds of years prior through organizations like Aspira and LULAC.

Under the banner of independence from colonial exploitation, economic underdevelopment, and institutional racism, the Chicano/Latino Civil Rights Movement had the central goals of land restoration, farm workers' rights, voting rights, and educational reform (Mariscal, 2005; Pedraza & Rivera, 2006). Ultimately, the Chicano/Latinx Civil Rights Movement marked a dramatic difference in the position of Latinx people in the U.S. with significant contributions to identity, the arts, activist culture, gender identity, and workplace defense (Mariscal, 2005). In fact, its collective actions resulted in the passing of the Bilingual Education Act of 1968 and the Equal Opportunity Act of 1974, both of which mandated the adoption of bilingual education programs in public schools (Gándara & Aldana, 2014). However, despite the adoption of these laws, English-only policies and attitudes and myopic discussions about race and language persist in public schools today (Paris & Alim, 2017a; Paris & Ball, 2009).

Culturally sustaining pedagogies carry on the work of the Black and Chicano/Latino Civil Rights Movements; interrogating "one-to-one" mapping of language and race solely focused on "static relationships between race, ethnicity, language, and cultural ways of being" (Alim & Paris, 2017, p. 7) while foregrounding bi/multilingual students' heritage language(s) and culture (Paris & Alim, 2014, 2017a). Parallel to the insurgence of these Black and Latinx movements, leaders of the American Indian Movement guided Indigenous American people to "re-create a type of society for themselves that can defy, mystify, and educate the rest of American society" to give "a new sense of conflict to Indian affairs" (Deloria, 1969, p. 252). During the 1960s and 1970s Indigenous American people mobilized to forefront inequities affecting them through grassroots efforts aimed at "bringing together tradition and pragmatic politics in such as areas as substance abuse, tribal government, and education" (Warrior, 1995, p. 95). The American Indian or Native Rights Movement, formally founded in July 1968, demanded attention to unsafe living conditions and generations of exploitation and neglect by federal and local agencies. The American Indian Movement's collective 1970 occupation of Wounded Knee, the sight of the 1890 massacre described earlier, was one of over 70 such occupations of symbols of Indigenous oppression, including Mount Rushmore, the Bureau of Indian Affairs building in Washington, D.C., and the replica of the Mayflower in Plymouth, MA (Bancroft, Wittstock, & Tum, 2013). Protesters used the occupations to call attention to Indigenous rights and demand that the government honor its treaty obligations (Bancroft et al., 2013). Such occupations led to legal actions against and jailing of many leaders of this movement (Warrior, 1995). The Civil Rights struggles of Indigenous people, and in particular the need for tribal sovereignty and language preservation, persist in the work of many who still fight for Indigenous peoples' rights, including those implementing asset-based and culturally revitalizing pedagogies in Indigenous communities (Lee & McCarty, 2017).

Branches: Asset-Based Theories and Pedagogies

Asset-based theories and pedagogies focus on building and extending from children's cultural and linguistic assets. They position cultural communities as "a coordinated group of people with some traditions and understandings in common, extending across several generations, with varied roles and practices and continual change among participants as well as transformation in the community's practices" (Gutiérrez & Rogoff, 2003, p. 21). Such bodies of work include sociocultural theory (Cole, 1995; Gutiérrez & Rogoff, 2003; Rogoff, 2003; Vygotsky, 1978), multicultural education (Abrahams & Troike, 1972; Banks & Banks, 2009; Forbes, 1973), funds of knowledge (González, Moll, & Amanti, 2005; Gutiérrez & Johnson, 2017), and third space approaches to teaching and learning (Gutiérrez, Baquedano-López, & Tejada, 1999; Gutiérrez & Johnson, 2017). Asset-based theories seek understandings about how people live culturally and how they organize their socioculturally formed "repertoires of practice—that is, the ways of engaging in activities stemming from participation in a range of cultural practices, as well as the learning that occurs in the development of those repertoires" (Gutiérrez & Johnson, 2017, p. 251). Briefly overviewed below, these bodies of thought situate the "linguistic, literate, and cultural practices of working-class communities—specifically poor communities of color" as resources and assets to "honor, explore, and extend" (Paris & Alim, 2014, p. 87).

Sociocultural Theories

Sociocultural theories forward that children learn everything first on a social/interactive plane and then relegate knowledge to internal thought. Central to sociocultural theory is Vygotsky's (1978) notion of zones of proximal development as places where two or more learners interact with each other or where learners interact with texts and thereby go beyond what they could accomplish on their own as a central concept of sociocultural theory. Vygotsky's (1978) theory points to important links between culture, cognition, and memory. Sociocultural theories help us understand learning as an ecologically mediated, socially constructed activity where children use languages and other tools to regulate, negotiate, and express relationships between themselves and in connection with their learning (Cole, 1995; Lee, 2017; Genishi & Dyson, 2009; Gregory, Long, & Volk, 2004). Rogoff (1999) describes learners in these spaces as moving in and out of roles of novice and expert depending on the turn of the conversation or interaction.

Sociocultural theorists have also illuminated funds of knowledge in homes and communities that many teachers consider to be void of language and knowledge (González et al., 2005). Funds of knowledge frameworks call for teachers to draw from a "network of practices that are part of people's everyday lives" (Gutiérrez & Johnson, 2017, p. 252) to teach as well as build students' confidence in their own knowledge and abilities. The concept of funds of knowledge is rooted in

Luis Moll, Cathy Amanti, Deborah Neff, and Norma González's (1992) study of Latinx communities' ways of knowing. They focused on how teachers can recognize and curricularly center the socially and culturally developed "funds of knowledge" or "the skills and knowledge that have been historically and culturally developed to enable an individual or household to function within a given culture" (p. 131) that are part of children's and families' everyday lives. In addition, Gregory et al. (2004) introduced the use of *syncretism* as an important window into students' expertise in drawing on home and community knowledge to create new and blended spaces for teaching and learning.

Third Space

Gutiérrez et al.'s (1999) work with Latinx students from migrant families regards *third spaces* as "collective zones of proximal development" (Gutiérrez & Johnson, 2017, p. 252) where students negotiate different forms of academic, social, cultural, and epistemological tension or conflict leading to positive outcomes (Gutiérrez et al., 1999). Third spaces are particular kinds of systems within zones of proximal development where children can develop "a new social imagination in which they can engage in historicized, sociocritical, and syncretic processes of reframing their cultural past as a resource in the present and a tool for future action" (Gutiérrez & Johnson, 2017, pp. 252–253).

Multicultural Education

Building conceptually from sociocultural theories, during the 1970s and 1980s, multicultural education developed out of lingering concern for racial and ethnic inequities that remained apparent in learning opportunities and outcomes for students of Color. Multicultural education scholars and practitioners recommended that teachers learn to draw on the cultures of racially and ethnically diverse students in their classrooms (Abrahams & Troike, 1972; Banks & Banks, 2009; Forbes, 1973; Nieto, 1992), asserting the psychological benefits of doing so (Chun-Hoon, 1973). Mohatt and Erickson (1981) found that teachers who had a "culturally congruent" (p. 107) style of interaction with their students were more effective in general. Aragon (1973), Cuban (1972), Foster (1993), and Gee (1985) focused on instructional strategies that emphasized inquiry, critique, and analysis of language as a social practice. Many researchers (Bishop, 1990; Delpit, 1988; Gay, 1997; Hollins, King, & Hayman, 1994; Irvine, 1990; Nieto, 1992) further developed these ideas, asserting that culturally diverse students' failure in school also stemmed from a lack of self-representation in texts (Bishop, 1990), societal conflict, and power struggles on the part of White teachers and their lack of education about the histories and cultural contributions of people of Color.

Collectively, the "branches" of asset-based theories (sociocultural theory, third space and syncretic approaches, and multicultural education) help educators understand that learning is mediated by and contextualized within and across languages and cultures. However, asset-based theories and pedagogies are not enough unless they lead us to take up specific pedagogies that critically center family and community ways of knowing and disrupt the teaching of White, Christian, English-only, heteronormative ways of being as normalized, while dismissing, distorting, and/or marginalizing communities and histories of peoples of Color. For example, Long, Volk, Baines, and Tisdale (2013) offered the notion of *critical syncretism* to insist on "attention to power structures that silence some ways of learning and teaching while privileging others" (p. 419) when accessing assets-based approaches.

Leaves and Fruit

The leaves and fruit of our metaphorical family tree illustrate fruition. By naming pedagogies which increasingly move towards sustenance of culture, or heritage and community practices, as leaves and fruits, we illustrate our belief that such pedagogies grow from a strong network of roots, solid trunk, and healthy branches described in the previous sections. While pedagogies noted in the trunk of the tree are termed asset or asset-based pedagogies, we do not use the term *asset pedagogies* to describe those pedagogies delineated as leaves and fruits. Paris and Alim (2014) push against notions of asset-based pedagogies "paying particular attention to asset pedagogy's failures to remain dynamic and critical" (p. 85). They critique three themes: (a) previous conceptions of asset pedagogies; (b) asset pedagogies that focus on heritage and community practices without noting how these practices change and grow contemporarily; and (c) the idea that asset-based pedagogies do not deal with "problematic elements expressed in some youth cultural practices" (p. 85). Instead they refer to heritage and community practices (p. 88). They argue that, while extremely challenging for educators, culturally sustaining pedagogies that stem from heritage and community practices address their areas of critique to "focus on sustaining pluralism through education ... and change in ways that previous iterations of asset pedagogies did not" (p. 88). As such, we discuss four related pedagogical approaches: culturally relevant, responsive, mediated, and sustaining teaching, as the leaves and fruit nurtured by the growth of this family tree.

Culturally Relevant Teaching

We see culturally relevant pedagogies as vehicles for countering oppressive and colonizing messages that children receive through Eurocratic practices (King & Swartz, 2015, 2018). Eurocratic practices result when a European worldview, which tends to value competition, individualism, and survival, is imposed through "officially sanctioned constraints ... on knowledge and systems [like education] that maintain [Euro]American authority and hegemony" (King & Swartz, 2018, p. 13).

We use the term Eurocratic, rather than Eurocentric, to denote that curriculum does not merely center oppressive and colonizing messages through European models, histories, and languages, but that this centering is officially sanctioned, required, and mandated in the Eurocratic ways of thinking that assume single truths grounded in European versions of the world's accomplishments, histories, and governmental structures.

Ladson-Billings (2009) came to her conceptualization of culturally relevant teaching while studying characteristics of effective teachers, described in her book *The Dreamkeepers: Successful Teachers of African American Children*. As noted earlier in this text, culturally relevant teaching focuses on three elements: student achievement, cultural competence, and developing a critical consciousness (Ladson-Billings, 2017). Culturally relevant pedagogies use knowledge of students' cultures to create curriculum where students can critically examine, question, and critique educational content. Culturally relevant teaching (CRT) "empower[s] students … to examine critically educational content and process and ask what its role is in creating a truly democratic and multicultural society" (Ladson-Billings, 1992, p. 106). The end result focuses on maintaining the student's culture in order to "transcend the negative effects of the dominant culture" (Ladson-Billings, 1995, p. 474) by both "understand[ing] and critique[ing] the existing social order" (Ladson-Billings, 1995, p. 474). The first action of culturally relevant teaching, academic achievement, has evolved since its original conception (Ladson-Billings, 2006). Ladson-Billings clarified that the outcomes of culturally relevant teaching do not define achievement narrowly with student test scores, but instead look to the empowerment of students, incorporation and maintenance of students' cultures, and creation of a high-quality learning environment (Ladson-Billings, 2014, 2017). Ladson-Billings (2017) later clarified the "most misunderstood" component of CRT, cultural competence, forefronting that it is "more than a list of 'do's and don'ts'" (p. 144) for those who work with people who are different from "the mainstream" (p. 144). In addition, Ladson-Billings (2017) describes the "neglected dimension" of culturally relevant teaching, sociopolitical or critical consciousness. Ladson-Billings (2017) calls the development of sociopolitical or critical consciousness the "so what?" of culturally relevant teaching. Teachers who develop students' sociopolitical and critical consciousness "work hard to help students engage in meaningful projects that solve problems that matter in their lives … [and] allows them to question the veracity of … classrooms" (pp. 145–146).

Culturally Responsive Teaching

Geneva Gay's (2002) conception of culturally responsive teaching centers on teaching that increases achievement, critical consciousness, and knowledge of self and culture (Gay, 2010; Howard & Terry, 2011). It asks teachers to use "the cultural characteristics, experiences, and perspectives of ethnically diverse students as conduits for teaching them more effectively" (Gay, 2002, p. 106). Culturally responsive pedagogies are grounded in the concern that students who struggle the most in schools are those whose discursive styles are outside the dominant culture (Rueda, 2011). Rather than expect students from culturally and linguistically diverse backgrounds to assimilate or approximate dominant culture, Gay (2010) argues for "a very different pedagogical paradigm … one that teaches to and through [students'] personal and cultural strengths" (p. 24). Carol Lee's (2001) cultural modeling is an example of culturally responsive teaching, as teachers scaffold African American students' understanding of literary text through building on students' language and discourse patterns. Like culturally relevant pedagogies, culturally responsive teaching begins with cultural congruence and turns to action: situating the experiences of students within the curriculum to increase motivation, engagement, and appeal (Gay, 2002).

Culturally Mediated Instruction

Hollins (2015) describes culturally mediated instruction as applying culturally mediated cognition, culturally appropriate social learning spaces, and culturally valued understanding in curriculum (p. 156). In authentic culturally mediated instruction "schooling practices are an extension of the enculturation process found in the child's home and local community" (p. 157). Culturally mediated instruction requires that teachers develop an understanding of students' ways of knowing and being (Hollins, 2015). Ultimately, culturally relevant, responsive, and mediated teaching pivot around *what is working* with students of Color, instead of what is not (Ladson-Billings, 2014).

Culturally Sustaining Pedagogies

Culturally sustaining pedagogies draw foundationally on, expand, and critique the definitive goals of culturally relevant teaching and other asset-based frameworks, theories, and pedagogies. Culturally sustaining pedagogies require teachers to "be more than responsive or relevant" (Paris, 2012, p. 95) by dedicating to *sustaining* the plurality of identities and cultures while recognizing the agency of children to confront oppressive messages even while they may have internalized those messages (Gutiérrez & Johnson, 2017). Thus, a key difference from culturally relevant and responsive teaching is the focus on *sustaining practices*—not merely teaching a culturally relevant lesson or unit of study, but institutionalizing this kind of teaching as the pedagogical norm *and* in so doing, moving toward sustaining cultural and linguistic strengths in the lives of students and society. Offering "loving critiques" of Ladson-Billings's (1995) ideas, Paris's (2012) concept of CSP asks not only *what is the purpose of schooling?* but *what is the purpose of schooling in pluralistic societies?* (Alim & Paris, 2017, pp. 1–3). The culturally sustaining response to these questions is that educational environments must not only honor "youth heritage practices and community engagements, but also provide students with access to opportunity and power … [with a focus on eradicating] oppressive, racist educational policies that advantage monoculturalism" (Kinloch, 2017, p. 29). Thus, CSP critically centers multilingual and multicultural heritage and community practices through actively building on student and community input, linking community practices with past and present (Paris & Alim, 2017b); focuses on raising students' abilities to critique dominant messages and regressive practices that privilege White, middle-class norms even as they enact such practices within their own communities (2017b); and requires teachers to develop the capacity to apply these characteristics to their own practice. At its core, however, CSP is not just about embracing these tenets at a moment-in-time but as a radical act "that disrupts a schooling system centered on ideologies of White, middle class, monolingual, cisheteropatriarchal, able-bodied superiority" (Paris & Alim, 2017b, p. 13).

This move is crucial, as schooling has historically functioned as a space that erases and diminishes "the expansive contributions, heritage, intellect, and expertise of those who were enslaved or colonized" (Long et al., 2016, p. 14) and their descendants. This move to not only embrace but sustain multiculturalism and a balance of power in a multicultural society is also important because it provides educational breadth and depth for students from dominant cultural groups who will otherwise grow up seeing *their* heritage as that which drives the world's knowledge (Baines et al., 2018). Culturally sustaining pedagogies work to decenter Whiteness (Alim & Paris, 2017; Kinloch, 2017), requiring a "reframe[ing of] what we think about the students and their homes, as well as how we view ourselves, our social identities and our roles in this process" (Boutte, 2015, p. 3). Beginning with "the knowledge that our languages, literacies, histories, and cultural ways of being as people and communities of color are not pathological" (Alim & Paris, 2017, p. 2), CSP asks:

> What if the goal of teaching and learning with youth of color was not ultimately to see how closely students could perform White middle-class norms, but rather was to explore, honor, extend, and at times, problematize their cultural practices and investments? (p. 3)

Paris and Alim (2017b) forward that, in educational practice, CSP involves:

1. A critical centering on dynamic community languages, valued practices, and knowledges [that must be] centered meaningfully;
2. Student and community agency and input (community accountability);
3. Historicized content and instruction [that] connect[s] present learning to the histories of racial, ethnic, and linguistic communities, and to the histories of neighborhood and cities, and the histories of the larger states and nation-states that they are a part of;

4. A capacity to contend with internalized oppressions [and counter messages and systems that suggest that marginalized students and families are the problem and value White, middle-class, monolingual, monocultural values above all else];
5. An ability to curricularize these features in learning settings.

Paris (2012) is clear that these pedagogical characteristics are not enough, also asserting the necessity of overturning and replacing institutional policies and practices that maintain the "quite explicit goal of creating a monocultural and monolingual society based on White, middle class norms of language and cultural being" (p. 95). To start this process, Paris and Alim (2017b) urge educators to interrogate their own teaching and educational institutions, asking questions that we paraphrase below:

- What do we seek to sustain?
- How does that influence what we decide to read, write, perform, and teach and in what classroom settings?
- Who are the sources of knowledge we must be in conversation with?
- How am I critically learning with a community?

Methodology: A Humanizing Approach to Our Work as Teacher-Researchers

Guided by the previously described family lineage, all of the dyads whose work is presented in the chapters that follow developed classroom practices and methods for studying those practices based on strong convictions that teaching and research should be humanizing. This means that the researcher must constantly question whose interests and needs are being served by the research and what change, if any, is being made within the context as a result. Thus, the research presented in this book is grounded in a humanizing framework (Bartolome, 1994; del Carmen Salazar, 2013; Paris & Winn, 2013). This framework takes into account the fact that much of educational research has a long history of *colonizing* and pathologizing communities of Color (Bartolome, 1994; Patel, 2015). In contrast, humanizing approaches seek to *decolonize* research, always asking: Who will the research benefit? (Madison, 2012; Smith, 2013) and "critical for whom?" because not asking "would be equivalent to colonizing participants—or, at the very least, to ethnocentrically imposing our own understandings, assumptions and experiences upon them" (Souto-Manning, 2013, p. 201). In morally driven commitments to conducting humanizing, decolonizing research, the dyads became co-researchers motivated to reach justice-oriented solutions that benefit children, schools, classrooms, families, and communities who have been historically marginalized.

A humanizing research framework insists on "relationships of care and dignity and dialogic consciousness raising" (Paris & Winn, 2013, p. xvi). This framework was exemplified as co-researchers (PDCRT dyads): a) engaged constantly in conversations about both how and what was happening in order to negotiate meaning about the data; b) reflected on their own and others' assumptions; c) used humanizing methodological approaches; d) worked to break down and blur boundaries between universities and schools; and e) challenged boundaries in research by reinvigorating multiple methods, including mixed methods, within qualitative research (Lincoln & Guba, 1999; Madison, 2012; Patel, 2015).

Research Question and Data Collection

Dyads focused on a central research question: *How can we critically reframe early literacy education by researching, creating, and exploring culturally relevant (and ultimately culturally sustaining) literacy practices through ongoing investigations in early childhood classrooms?* Our goals were connected to the three central objectives of the PDCRT as noted, to: deepen teacher/student critical consciousness; validate sociocultural, racial, and linguistic diversity as foundational to teaching; and support children most often marginalized in schools.

Collecting data for two years, dyads invented, reinvented, and borrowed from established data collection methods including: memoing, field notes, classroom photographs and video and audio recordings, teaching/learning artifacts such as children's work, lesson plans, interviews with children, family members, teachers, and community members, and records of each dyad's critical dialogue during weekly, monthly, and annual meetings. Through frequent critical conversations within and across dyads, we examined ourselves constantly to consider reciprocity, mutual respect, dialogue, and the interplay between ourselves, the critical theories that drove us, and our teaching and research methods (Bakhtin, 2010; Conquergood, 2013; Madison, 2012). Our work in classrooms demanded constant reflection on our ethical responsibility: the recognition that all of us are in the process of "becoming fully human" (Freire, 1983, p. 43) and that our words and our actions are part of an "intricate web of actions and inactions" that can tear, pull, or maintain tension within the web (Alcoff, 1991–1992, p. 20). From prekindergarten (three- and four-year-olds) to third-grade classroom contexts in New York, North Carolina, South Carolina, and Kansas, we considered our work as rooted in theories and methods that challenge "regimes of power" (Madison, 2012, p. 10).

Introducing the Dyads and their Approaches to Research

Preissle (2011) likens qualitative research to a "bramble bush of disciplinary roots, stems, and branches contributing to qualitative methods and methodologies" (p. 688). This aligns beautifully with the family tree metaphor that guides us. Our work to develop and document classroom practices drew not only from the legacy of critical educators and our theoretical family tree but also from a "bramble bush" of research methods including: critical ethnography, narrative, and phenomenological approaches, constructivist grounded theory, and practitioner inquiry methods. This bramble bush of methods helped us, across and within dyads, to unearth and analyze the stories that this book shares.

Patricia Piña and Kindel Nash (Chapter Two) worked together in Kansas City, Kansas in Patricia's pre-kindergarten (three- and four-year-olds) bilingual classroom. They centered their research in critical ethnographic methods as a way to understand and respond to the lived experiences of children and families within that particular cultural context. They did so by entering and becoming a part of that context; a process where "belonging precede[s] being" (Madison, 2012, p. 16). Put another way, Piña and Nash worked as a team within the classroom community, with Nash contributing to the life of the classroom as much as Piña, instead of taking a traditional researcher-role and sitting in the corner taking notes.

Mary Jade Haney and Julia López-Robertson (Chapter Three) used phenomenological and narrative research, focusing on the "content of stories people tell that help them make sense of their lived experiences" (Rossman & Rallis, 1998, p. 73) to support their work with PreK–Grade three students and their families in Columbia, South Carolina. Through Mary Jade's role as the school's reading specialist, they worked with students and families—Latina mothers and their children as well as African American children and families. They drew from *testimonio*, a research method that emerged from Latina critical race theory (Solorzano & Delgado Bernal, 2001), which rejects widely accepted conventions about what constitutes knowledge and foregrounds "lived realities that would otherwise succumb to the alchemy of erasure" (The Latina Feminist Group, 2001, p. 2).

Alicia Arce-Boardman and Bilal Polson (Chapter Four) used practitioner inquiry, drawn from action research methods, in Uniondale, Long Island, New York to learn about second- and third-graders' contexts, knowledge, and expertise, engage in reflective practice, and monitor changes in instructional practice and influence on students' learning (Mills, 2011). While action research is a systematic inquiry conducted by various stakeholders of a school community to learn about how the school operates, exploring the instructional practices of the teachers and the learning practices of the students (Mills, 2011), practitioner inquiry is an approach within action research that facilitates teachers-as-researchers who enhance their teaching and their students' experiences (Pine, 2008; Stringer, 2013; Wall & Hall, 2017).

Constructivist grounded theory (Charmaz, 1990, 2006, 2011) guided the work of Chinyere Harris and Crystal Glover (Chapter Five) as they used mixed methods to collect and interpret both qualitative and quantitative data from Chinyere's fourth- and later second-grade classrooms. Their work was anchored in this methodology because it "places priority on the phenomena of study and sees both data and analysis as created from shared experiences and relationships with participants and other sources of data" (Charmaz, 2006, p. 130), depending on, "not standing outside of, the researchers' views" (p. 130).

Chapter Six, written by Dinah Volk and Erin Miller, provides a synthesis of the practices described in Chapters Two through Five in order to better understand how these practices might manifest in every educator's professional space. In order to provide a context for those practices, Chapter Six shares the goals of the PDCRT project based on retrospective interviews with the project originators and first board members (Susi Long, Erin Miller, Dinah Volk, Mariana Souto-Manning, Eileen Blanco-Dougherty, Carmen Tisdale, Julia López-Robertson, and Bilal Polson). This chapter also describes the PDCRT's commitment to the work and creating spaces for leadership of educators of Color as a primary commitment of the project. This is particularly important since the chapter is written by Dinah Volk and Erin Miller, who describe their positionality as White women as important to this work in the commitment to leadership and policy change within the field of early childhood literacy broadly and NCTE specifically.

An Invitation

Paris and Alim (2014) urge us to "move forward, with love" (p. 95) as we recreate and recast notions of what culturally sustaining pedagogies might look like in early childhood settings. Given descriptions of the theories and research methods that form the foundation of our work, we invite you to move forward, with love, into this book. As early childhood educators, we deeply understand the need for edifying examples of teaching and assessment that critically center family and community ways of knowing over Eurocratic practices, strive to disrupt colonized histories, and showcase opportunities for children and families to confront oppressive and colonizing messages. To contribute to that work, each chapter of this book:

1. Highlights practices developed primarily by teachers of Color.
2. Showcases practices and assessments that privilege young children and communities of Color (preK–3).
3. Demonstrates the impact of practices by providing literacy achievement data from children in dyad classrooms and schools.
4. Shares the process (challenges, successes, strategies) of developing teacher–teacher educator partnerships as mutual-learning relationships, re-envisioning thinking about university–school partnerships.
5. Discusses challenges met (individual, institutional, professional, personal) in the work to develop and implement practices including strategies for negotiating those challenges.

Join us in exploring pedagogies and mutual learning partnerships that honor children and communities, as "a radical act" made possible by centuries of struggle (Paris & Alim, 2017b, p. 13). Returning to the wisdom of Anna Julia Cooper, we encourage you to move forward with this book as a tool to understand that "education for the human soul ... give[s] power and the right direction to the intellect, the sensibilities, and the will" (Cooper, 1892, p. 252). Join us as we "move forward, with love," exploring pedagogies and learning partnerships that represent "explicit resistances," recognizing that without such resistances children "will continue the age-old American saga of being asked to lose their heritage and community ways with language, literacy, and culture in order to achieve in U.S. schools" (Paris, 2012, p. 95). We move forward, with love, honoring children and seeking pedagogical and institutional change that keeps this kind of teaching from being outside the norm, tentative, or temporary.

Notes

1 We capitalize all racial and ethnic identifiers (White, Black/African American, Latinx, people of Color) in this volume unless we quote another author who did not choose to do so.
2 We use the words Black and African American interchangeably, reflecting prevalent ways that the Black/African American community names itself.
3 Recognizing the complexity of the term, we use *Latinx* here as an inclusive, gender-neutral way to describe Latino/a communities and disrupt traditional understandings of intersectional identity (Salinas & Lozano, 2019). It is not uncommon in communities of Color for people to use various terms to refer to themselves—sometimes interchangeably (Latinx and Latino/a or African American and Black or Indigenous, Indian, and Native). Thus, some authors featured in the book/participants in this project do not use *Latinx* as they self-identify as Latina or Latino. We view the use of these varying identifications as indicative of the sophistication and advancement of cultures, nationalities, and identities.

References

Abrahams, R., & Troike, R. (Eds.) (1972). *Language and cultural diversity in American education*. Englewood Cliffs, NJ: Prentice Hall.

Alcoff, L. (1991–1992). The problem of speaking for others. *Cultural Critique*, 20, 5–32.

Alim, H. S., & Paris, D. (2015). Whose language gap? Critical and culturally sustaining pedagogies as necessary challenges to racializing hegemony. *Journal of Linguistic Anthropology*, 25, 79–81.

Alim, H. S., & Paris, D. (2017). What is culturally sustaining pedagogy and why does it matter? In D. Paris & H. S. Alim (Eds.), *Culturally sustaining pedagogies: Teaching and learning for justice in a changing world* (pp. 1–24). New York, NY: Teachers College Press.

Anzaldúa, G. (1999). *Borderlands La Frontera*. San Francisco, CA: Aunt Lute Books.

Appiah, K. A., & Gates Jr, H. L. (Eds.). (2005). *Africana: The encyclopedia of the African and African American experience*. New York, NY: Oxford University Press.

Aragon, J. (1973). An impediment to cultural pluralism: Culturally deficient educators attempting to teach culturally different children. In M. D.Stent, W. R.Hazard, & H. N. Rivlin (Eds.), *Cultural pluralism in education: A mandate for change* (pp.77–84). New York, NY: Appleton-Century-Crofts.

Asante, M. K. (1992). *Kemet, Afrocentricity and knowledge*. Trenton, NJ: Africa World Press.

Asante, M. K. (2012). The character of Kwame Nkrumah's united Africa vision. *Journal of Pan African Studies*, 4(9), 12–26.

Au, K. H. (1979). Using the Experience-Text Relationship method with Minority Children. *The Reading Teacher*, 31, 46–49.

Baines, J., Tisdale, C., & Long, S. (2018). *"We've been doing it your way long enough": Choosing the culturally relevant classroom*. New York, NY: Teachers College Press.

Bakhtin, M. M. (2010). *The dialogic imagination: Four essays* (Vol. 1). Austin, TX: University of Texas Press.

Baldwin, J. (2013). *The fire next time*. New York, NY: Vintage.

Ball, A. F. (1995). Text design patterns in the writing of urban African American students; Teaching to the cultural strengths of students in multicultural settings. *Urban Education*, 30, 253–289.

Bancroft, D., Wittstock, L. W., & Tum, R. M. (2013). *We are still here: A photographic history of the American Indian movement*. St. Paul, MN: Minnesota Historical Society.

Banks, J. A., & Banks, C. A. M. (2009). *Multicultural education: Issues and perspectives*. New York, NY: John Wiley & Sons.

Bartolome, L. (1994). Beyond the methods fetish: Toward a humanizing pedagogy. *Harvard Educational Review*, 64, 173–195.

Behnken, B. D., Smithers, G. D., & Wendt, S. (Eds.). (2017). *Black intellectual thought in modern America: A historical perspective*. Jackson, MS: University Press of Mississippi.

Bell, D. (2004). *Silent covenants: Brown v. Board of Education and the unfulfilled hopes for racial reform*. New York, NY: Oxford University Press.

Bell, D. A. (1992). Racial realism. *Connecticut Law Review*, 24(79), 363–374.

Bishop, R. S. (1990). Mirrors, windows, and sliding glass doors. *Perspectives*, 6(3), ix–xi. Retrieved from https://scenicregional.org/wp-content/uploads/2017/08/Mirrors-Windows-and-Sliding-Glass-Doors.pdf

Bonilla-Silva, E. (2006). *Racism without racists: Color-blind racism and the persistence of racial inequality in the United States*. Lanham, MD: Rowman & Littlefield Publishers.

Boutte, G. S. (2015). *Educating African American students: And how are the children?*London: Routledge.

Bucholtz, M., Casillas, D. I., & Lee, J. S. (2017). Language and culture as sustenance. In D. Paris & H. S. Alim (Eds.), *Culturally sustaining pedagogies: Teaching and learning for justice in a changing world* (pp.43–59). New York, NY: Teachers College Press.

Charmaz, K. (1990). 'Discovering' chronic illness: Using grounded theory. *Social Science & Medicine*, 30, 1161–1172.

Charmaz, K. (2006). *Constructing grounded theory: A practical guide through qualitative analysis*. Thousand Oaks, CA: Sage.

Charmaz, K. (2011). Grounded theory methods in social justice research. In N. K. Denzin & Y. Lincoln (Eds.), *The Sage handbook of qualitative research* (4th ed., pp. 359–380). Thousand Oaks, CA: Sage.

Chun-Hoon, L. (1973). Jade Snow Wong and the fate of Chinese–American identity. In S. Sue & N. Wagner (Eds.), *Asian-Americans: Psychological perspectives* (pp.125–135). Ben Lomond, CA: Science and Behavior Books.

Cole, M. (1995). Socio-cultural-historical psychology: Some general remarks and a proposal for a new kind of cultural-genetic methodology. In J. V. Wertsch, P. del Río, & A. Alvarez (Eds.), *Learning in doing: Social, cognitive, and computational aspects. Sociocultural studies of mind* (pp.187–214). New York, NY: Cambridge University Press.

Conquergood, D. (2013). *Cultural struggles: Performance, ethnography, praxis*. Detroit, MI: University of Michigan Press.

Cooper, A. J. (1892). *A voice from the south: By a black woman of the south*. Xenia, OH: The Aldine Printing House.

Cuban, L. (1972). Ethnic content and white instruction. *The Phi Delta Kappan*, 53, 270–273.

Delany, M. R. (1879). *Principia of ethnology: The origin of races and color*. Whitefish, MT: Kessinger Publications.

del Carmen Salazar, M. (2013). A humanizing pedagogy: Reinventing the principles and practice of education as a journey toward liberation. *Review of Research in Education*, 37, 121–148.

Deloria, V. (1969). *Custer died for your sins: An Indian manifesto*. New York, NY: Macmillan Company.

Delpit, L. (1988). The silenced dialogue: Power and pedagogy in educating other people's children. *Harvard Educational Review*, 58, 280–299.

Diop, C. A. (1991). *Civilization or barbarism*. Chicago, IL: Chicago Review Press.

DuBois, W. E. B. (1898/2001). *The education of Black people: Ten critiques, 1906–1960*. New York, NY: NYU Press.

Forbes, J. (1973). Teaching Native American values and cultures. In *43rd yearbook* (pp.201–225). Washington, DC: National Council for the Social Studies.

Foster, M. (1993) Educating for competence in community and culture: Exploring the views of exemplary African-American teachers, *Urban Education*, 27, 370–394.

Foster, M. (1997). *Black teachers on teaching*. New York, NY: New Press.

Freire, P. (1970, 1983, 2000, 2010). *Pedagogy of the oppressed*. New York, NY: The Continuum International Publishing Group.

Freire, P. (1972). Education: Domestication or liberation? *Prospects*, 2, 173–181.

Gándara, P. C., & Aldana, U. S. (2014). Who's Segregated now? Latinos, language, and the future of integrated schools. *Educational Administration Quarterly*, 50, 735–748.

Gay, G. (1997). Multicultural infusion in teacher education: Foundations and applications. In A. I. Morley & M. K. Kitano (Eds.), *Multicultural course transformation in higher education: A broader truth* (pp. 192–210). Boston, MA: Allyn & Bacon.

Gay, G. (2002). Preparing for culturally responsive teaching. *Journal of Teacher Education*, 53, 106–116.

Gay, G. (2010). *Culturally responsive teaching: Theory, research, and practice*. New York, NY: Teachers College Press.

Gee, J. P. (1985). The narrativization of experience in the oral style. *Journal of Education*, 167, 9–35. Genishi, C., & Dyson, A. H. (2009). *Children, language, and literacy: Diverse learners in diverse times*. New York, NY: Teachers College Press.

González, N., Moll, L. & Amanti, C. (Eds.). (2005). *Fund of knowledge: Theorizing practices in households and classrooms*. Mahwah, NJ: Erlbaum.

Grande, S. (2004, 2015). *Red pedagogy: Native American social and political thought*. New York, NY: Rowman & Littlefield.

Grant, C., Brown, K., & Brown, A. (2016). *Black intellectual thought in education: The missing traditions of Anna Julia Cooper, Carter G. Woodson, and Alain LeRoy Locke*. London: Routledge.

Gregory, E., Long, S., & Volk, D. (2004). *Many pathways to literacy: Young children learning with siblings, grandparents, peers, and communities*. London: Routledge.

Gutiérrez, K. D., Baquedano-López, P., & Tejada, C. (1999). Rethinking diversity: Hybridity and hybrid language practices in third space. *Mind, Culture, and Activity*, 6, 286–303.

Gutiérrez, K. D., & Johnson, P. (2017). Understanding identity sampling and cultural repertoires: Advancing learning in justice pedagogies. InD. Paris & H. S. Alim (Eds.), *Culturally sustaining pedagogies: Teaching and learning for justice in a changing world* (pp. 247–260). New York, NY: Teachers College Press.

Gutiérrez, K. D., & Rogoff, B. (2003). Cultural ways of learning: Individual traits or repertoires of practice. *Educational Researcher*, 32(5), 19–25.

Hollins, E. R. (2015). *Culture in school learning: Revealing the deep meaning*. London: Routledge.

Hollins, E. R., King, J., & Hayman, W. (1994). *Teaching diverse populations: Formulating a knowledge base*. New York, NY: SUNY Press.

hooks, b. (2014). *Teaching to transgress*. New York, NY: Routledge.

Howard, T., & Terry Sr, C. L. (2011). Culturally responsive pedagogy for African American students: Promising programs and practices for enhanced academic performance. *Teaching Education*, 22, 345–362.

Irizarry, J. G. (2017). "For us, by us": A vision for culturally sustaining pedagogies forwarded by Latinx youth. In D. Paris & H. S. Alim (Eds.), *Culturally sustaining pedagogies: Teaching and learning for justice in a changing world* (pp. 83–98). New York, NY: Teachers College Press.

Irvine, J. J. (1990). *Black students and school failure. Policies, practices, and prescriptions*. Westport, CT: Greenwood Press.

Irvine, J. J. (2003). *Educating teachers for diversity: Seeing with a cultural eye* (Vol. 15). New York, NY: Teachers College Press.

Johnson, R. C., Kalil, A., & Dunifon, R. E. (2010). *Mothers' work and children's lives: Low-income families after welfare reform*. Kalamazoo, MI: W.E. Upjohn Institute for Employment Research.

Joseph, P. E. (Ed.). (2006). *The black power movement: Rethinking the civil rights-black power era*. New York, NY: Taylor & Francis.

Kincheloe, J. L. (2008). *Critical pedagogy primer*. New York, NY: Peter Lang.

King, J. E. (Ed.). (2006). *Black education: A transformative research and action agenda for the new century*. New York, NY: Routledge.

King, J. E., & Swartz, E. E. (2015). *The Afrocentric praxis of teaching for freedom: Connecting culture to learning*. New York, NY: Routledge.

King, J. E., & Swartz, E. E. (2018). *Heritage knowledge in the curriculum: Retrieving an African episteme*. London: Routledge.

King, P. J. (2016). *The truth about the Wounded Knee Massacre*. Retrieved from https://newsmaven.io/indiancountrytoday/archive/the-truth-about-the-wounded-knee-massacre-PIQqUKeCEEmnLeQn0Q5SOQ

Kinloch, V. (2017). "You ain't making me write." In D. Paris & H. S. Alim (Eds.), *Culturally sustaining pedagogies: Teaching and learning for justice in a changing world* (pp. 25–43). New York, NY: Teachers College Press.

Kinloch, V. (2011). Reflecting on cultivating new voices among scholars of Color. *English Journal*, 101, 83–85. Ladson-Billings, G. (1992). Culturally relevant teaching: The key to making multicultural education work. In C. A. Grant (Ed.), *Research and multicultural education: From the margins to the mainstream* (pp. 102–118). Bristol, PA: The Falmer Press.

Ladson-Billings, G. (1995). Toward a theory of culturally relevant pedagogy. *American Educational Research Journal*, 32, 465–491.

Ladson-Billings, G. (2006). From the achievement gap to the education debt: Understanding achievement in US schools. *Educational Researcher*, 35(7), 3–12.

Ladson-Billings, G. (2009). *The dreamkeepers: Successful teachers of African American children*. San Francisco, CA: Jossey-Bass.

Ladson-Billings, G. (2014). Culturally relevant pedagogy 2.0: a.k.a. the remix. *Harvard Educational Review*, 84, 74–84.

Ladson-Billings, G. (2017). The (r)evolution will not be standardized: Teacher education, hip hop pedagogy, and culturally relevant pedagogy 2.0. In D. Paris & H. S. Alim (Eds.), *Culturally sustaining pedagogies: Teaching and learning for justice in a changing world* (pp. 141–156). New York, NY: Teachers College Press.

Lee, C. D. (2001). Is October Brown Chinese? A cultural modeling activity system for underachieving students. *American Educational Research Journal*, 38, 97–141.

Lee, C. D. (2017). An ecological framework for enacting culturally sustaining pedagogy. In D. Paris & H. S. Alim (Eds.), *Culturally sustaining pedagogies: Teaching and learning for justice in a changing world* (pp. 261–274). New York, NY: Teachers College Press.

Lee, T., & McCarty, T. (2017). Upholding indigenous education sovereignty through critical culturally sustaining/revitalizing pedagogy. In D. Paris & H. S. Alim (Eds.), *Culturally sustaining pedagogies: Teaching and learning for justice in a changing world* (pp. 61–82). New York, NY: Teachers College Press.

Lemert, C., & Bhan, E. (1998). *The voice of Anna Julia Cooper*. Lanham, MD: Rowman & Littlefield Publishers.

Lincoln, Y. S., & Guba, E. G. (1999). *Naturalistic inquiry*. Beverly Hills, CA: SAGE Publications.

Lomawaima, K. T., & McCarty, T. L. (2006). *"To remain an Indian": Lessons in democracy from a century of Native American education*. New York, NY: Teachers College Press.

Long, S. (2011). *Supporting students in a time of core standards: English language arts, grades prek-2*. Urbana, IL: National Council of Teachers of English.

Long, S., Souto-Manning, M., & Vasquez, V. (2016). *Courageous leadership in early childhood education: Taking a stand for social justice*. New York, NY: Teachers College Press.

Long, S., Volk, D., Baines, J., & Tisdale, C. (2013). "We've been doing it your way long enough": Syncretism as a critical process. *Journal of Early Childhood Literacy*, 13, 418–439.

Lorde, A. (2007). *Sister outsider: Essays and speeches*. Berkeley, CA: Crossing.

Madison, D. S. (2012). *Critical ethnography: Method, ethics, and performance*. Thousand Oaks, CA: Sage.

Mariscal, G. (2005). *Brown-eyed children of the sun: Lessons from the Chicano movement, 1965–1975*. Alburquerque, NM: University of New Mexico Press.

Martínez, E. (2000). Seeing more than Black and White. In M. Adams, W. J. Blumenfeld, R. Castaneda, H. W. Hackman, M. L. Peters, & X. Zuniga (Eds.), *Readings for diversity and social justice* (pp.95–99). New York, NY: Psychology Press.

McCarty, T., & Lee, T. (2014). Critical culturally sustaining/revitalizing pedagogy and Indigenous education sovereignty. *Harvard Educational Review*, 84(1), 101–124.

McCoy, K., Tuck, E., & McKenzie, M. (Eds.). (2016). *Land education: Rethinking pedagogies of place from Indigenous, postcolonial, and decolonizing perspectives*. Abingdon:Routledge.

Meyer, G. J. (2011). Pedro Albizu Campos, Gilberto Concepcion de Gracia, and Vito Marcantonio's collaboration in the cause of Puerto Rico's independence. *Centro Journal*, 23, 87–123.

Miller, E. T. (2015). Race as the Benu: A reborn consciousness for teachers of our youngest children. *Journal of Curriculum Theorizing*, 30(3), 28–44.

Milner, H. R. (2008). Critical race theory and interest convergence as analytic tools in teacher education policies and practices. *Journal of Teacher Education*, 59, 332–346.

Mills, G. E. (2011). *Action research: A guide for the teacher researcher*. New York, NY: Pearson.

Mohatt, G., & Erickson, F. (1981). Cultural differences in teaching styles in an Odawa school: A sociolinguistic approach. In H. T. Trueba, G. Pung Guthrie, & K. H.-P. Au

(Eds.), *Culture and the bilingual classroom: Studies in classroom ethnography* (pp.105–135). Rowley, MA: Newbury House Publishers.

Moll, L. C., Amanti, C., Neff, D., & Gonzalez, N. (1992). Funds of knowledge for teaching: Using a qualitative approach to connect homes and classrooms. *Theory into Practice*, 31, 132–141.

Morrison, T. (1998, March). *From an interview on Charlie Rose*. Public Broadcasting Service. Retrieved from http://www.youtube.com/watch?v=F4vIGvKpT1c

National Center for Education Statistics. (2016). *The condition of education: Reading performance*. Retrieved from https://nces.ed.gov/programs/coe/indicator_cnb.asp

Navarro, S. A., & Mejia, A. X. (2004). *Latino Americans and political participation: A reference handbook*. Denver, CO: ABC-Clio.

Neihardt, J. G. (2014). *Black Elk speaks: The complete edition*. Lincoln, NE: Bison Books.

Nieto, S. (1992). *Affirming diversity: The sociopolitical context of multicultural education*. White Plains, NY: Longman.

Nuñez, L. (2009). Reflections on Puerto Rican history: Aspira in the sixties and the coming of age of the stateside Puerto Rican community. *Centro Journal*, 21, 33–47.

Ongiri, A. A. (2009). *Spectacular blackness: The cultural politics of the black power movement and the search for a black aesthetic*. Charlottesville, VA: University of Virginia Press.

Ostler, J. (2004). *The Plains Sioux and U.S. colonialism from Lewis and Clark to Wounded Knee*. Cambridge: Cambridge University Press.

Painter, N. I. (1996). *Sojourner Truth: A life, a symbol*. New York, NY: WW Norton & Company.

Paris, D. (2012). Culturally sustaining pedagogy: A needed change in stance, terminology, and practice. *Educational Researcher*, 41(3), 93–97.

Paris, D., & Alim, H. S. (2014). What are we seeking to sustain through culturally sustaining pedagogy? A loving critique forward. *Harvard Educational Review*, 84, 85–100.

Paris, D., & Alim, H. S. (2017a). *Author interview by Larry Ferlazzo: Culturally sustaining pedagogies*. Retrieved from http://blogs.edweek.org/teachers/classroom_qa_with_larry_ferlazzo/2017/07/author_interview_culturally_sustaining_pedagogies.html?r=604476754.

Paris, D., & Alim, H. S. (2017b). *Culturally sustaining pedagogies: Teaching and learning for justice in a changing world*. New York, NY: Teachers College Press.

Paris, D., & Ball, A. (2009). Teacher knowledge in culturally and linguistically complex classrooms: Lessons from the golden age and beyond. In L. M. Morrow, R. Rueda, & D. Lapp (Eds.), *Handbook of research on literacy instruction: Issues of diversity, policy, and equity* (pp. 379–395). New York, NY: Guilford Press.

Paris, D., & Winn, M. T. (Eds.). (2013). *Humanizing research: Decolonizing qualitative inquiry with youth and communities*. Thousand Oaks, CA: Sage Publications.

Patel, L. (2015). *Decolonizing educational research: From ownership to answerability*. London: Routledge.

Pedraza, P., & Rivera, M. (Eds.). (2006). *Latino education: An agenda for community action* research. London: Routledge. Pine, G. J. (2008). *Teacher action research: Building knowledge democracies*. Thousand Oaks, CA: Sage.

Preissle, J. (2011). Qualitative futures: Where we might go from where we've been. In N. K. Denzin & Y. Lincoln (Eds.), *The Sage handbook of qualitative research* (4th ed., pp. 685–698). Thousand Oaks, CA: Sage.

Rogoff, B. (1999). Cognitive development through social interaction: Vygotsky and Piaget. In P. Murphy (Ed.), *Learners, learning and assessment* (pp.69–82). London: Paul Chapman Publishing.

Rogoff, B. (2003). *The cultural nature of human development*. London: Oxford University Press.

Rossman, G. B., & Rallis, S. F. (1998). *Learning in the field: An introduction to qualitative research*. Thousand Oaks, CA: SAGE Publications.

Rueda, R. (2011). Cultural perspectives in reading: Theory and research. In R. Barr, M. L. Kamil, P. B. Mosenthal, & P. D. Pearson (Eds.), *Handbook of reading research, volume IV* (pp.110–130). New York, NY: Routledge.

Salinas Jr, C., & Lozano, A. (2019). Mapping and recontextualizing the evolution of the term Latinx: An environmental scanning in higher education. *Journal of Latinos and Education*, 18, 302–315.

Smith, L. T. (2013). *Decolonizing methodologies: Research and indigenous peoples*. London: Zed Books.

Solorzano, D. G., & Delgado Bernal, D. (2001). Examining transformational resistance through a critical race and latcrit theory framework: Chicana and Chicano students in an urban context. *Urban Education*, 36, 308–342.

Souto-Manning, M. (2013). *Multicultural teaching in the early childhood classroom: Approaches, strategies, and tools, preschool–2nd grade*. New York, NY: Teachers College Press.

Souto-Manning, M., & Martell, J. (2017). *Reading, writing, and talk: Inclusive teaching strategies for diverse learners, K–2*. New York, NY: Teachers College Press. Standing Bear, L. (1988). *My Indian boyhood*. Lincoln, NE: University of Nebraska Press. (Original work published 1931).

Stringer, E. T. (2013). *Action research*. Thousand Oaks, CA: Sage Publications.

The Latina Feminist Group. (2001). *Telling to live: Latina feminist testimonies*. Durham, NC: Duke University Press.

Theoharis, J. (2018). *A more beautiful and terrible history: The uses and misuses of civil rights history*. Boston, MA: Beacon Press.

Torres, R., & Vázquez, F. (2003). *Latinx thought: Culture, politics, and society*. London: Routledge.

Tuck, E., & McKenzie, M. (2015). Relational validity and the "where" of inquiry: Place and land in qualitative research. *Qualitative Inquiry*, 21, 633–638.

Vygotsky, L. S. (1978). *Mind in society*. Cambridge, MA: Harvard University Press.

Wall, K., & Hall, E. (2017). The teacher in teacher-practitioner research: Three principles of inquiry. In P. Boyd & A. Szplit (Eds.), *Teachers and teacher educators learning through inquiry: International perspectives* (pp.35–62). Krakow: Wydawnictwo Attyka. Retrieved from http://nrl.northumbria.ac.uk/id/eprint/31299

Warrior, R. A. (1995). *Tribal secrets: Recovering American Indian intellectual traditions*. Minneapolis, MN: University of Minnesota Press.

Woodson, C. G. (1933). *The mis-education of the Negro*. Trenton, NJ: Africa World Press.

2

TRANSLANGUAGING PEDAGOGIES IN A BILINGUAL PRESCHOOL CLASSROOM

Kindel Turner Nash and Iris Patricia Piña

It was 9:00 am on a Tuesday morning in early September. Kindel Nash stepped through the doorway into Patricia Piña's Spanish/English dual-language classroom at El Centro Academy for Children, where 70% of the learners were Latinx and learning English alongside their heritage languages. Sixteen three- and four-year-old students were engaged in free-choice center play. Three students were playing a letter-matching game on the computers, four children built a tower with Duplo blocks at a small rectangular table, a few students constructed a castle-like structure of wooden blocks in the carpeted area, two children stirred plastic grapes on the stove in the dramatic play area, and two more children were cutting pieces of paper at another table. The children talked to themselves and to each other, moving easily across Spanish and English languages, often using both languages within the same sentences. They followed the lead of their teacher, Ms. Iris (known as Patricia to her family and friends), who conversed fluidly across Spanish and English throughout the day. That morning, for example, she offered moment-to-moment guidance to Josué, who was cutting paper, "*Así, de esta manera*, hold it like this, watch me." Uzziel, a three-year-old boy, also traversed both Spanish and English as he approached Kindel as soon as she walked through the door, placing *Clifford el gran perro rojo/Clifford the Big Red Dog* (Bridwell, 2009) into her hands, exclaiming, "Vamos, read this one!" Kindel, as a developing bilingual, began to read the book in her emerging Spanish. This was the first day of our work together as a part of the Professional Dyads in Culturally Relevant Teaching (PDCRT) project. As a teacher–teacher educator dyad, we engaged together in studying, generating, and reflecting on culturally sustaining early literacy teaching practices in Patricia's classroom over a two-year period. After spending that first day immersed in Patricia's classroom, Kindel recorded a memo on her phone while driving home:

> I just had my first meeting at El Centro with Patricia, and, she told me all kinds of stories about herself and I'm just overwhelmed with excitement because my strongest feeling is that she already *gets* why we need to make our curriculum culturally relevant and our teaching culturally relevant, and she already *understands* and demonstrates the importance of the fluid use of Spanish and English in her classroom.

In this chapter, we (Patricia and Kindel) share aspects of our learning through engagement in the PDCRT project. The work in Patricia's language-rich classroom stands in stark contrast to the way early childhood pedagogy is typically represented—as a linear, stage-by-stage continuum of progression from one skill to the next. Yet, Kindel immediately witnessed Patricia's support for children's language and literacy learning as a complex, organic process with many simultaneous inputs and outputs (Genishi & Dyson, 2009; Genishi & Goodwin, 2008; Robinson & Yaden, 1993; Yaden et al., 2000; Yaden, 2013). Initially, we described Patricia's practices as culturally relevant, yet we have since come to adopt the term *culturally sustaining* as one that preserves the tenets of culturally relevant teaching while more clearly describing the way Patricia's practices were not just relevant to, but sustained, the children and families in her classroom and their languages and cultures during their time with her. In this chapter, we share elements of that process which include focusing on the culturally sustaining nature of Patricia's classroom practices with a particular focus on her use of translanguaging or "the planned and systematic use of two languages for teaching and learning inside the same lesson" (Williams, 1994, n.p.). We also share strategies that proved essential for nurturing our relationship as a teacher–teacher educator dyad negotiating challenges as we worked to bridge the divide between the preschool classroom and the university through our partnership. We offer our work to add to the growing body of research calling for a reconceptualization and decolonization of early language and literacy teaching, assessment, and partnering in multilingual contexts (Baines, Tisdale, & Long, 2018; Dyson, 2015; Hollins, 2015; Long, Volk, Baines, & Tisdale, 2013; Souto-Manning & Martell, 2016).

Meet the Authors and the El Centro Context

Patricia

Iris Patricia Piña self-identifies as Latina. At the time of this work, she was a bilingual (Spanish/English) early childhood classroom teacher, teaching in the bilingual preschool program at El Centro Academy for Children, where she had worked for seven years as a lead teacher, forming deep connections to the children, school, and broader community.

Patricia grew up in the Dominican Republic and moved to Kansas City, Kansas (where El Centro is located) when she was in high school. Patricia, who is Dominican and French, spoke of how she never felt that her Latinx culture was

FIGURE 2.1 Iris Patricia Piña.

acknowledged during her public school education in the Dominican Republic and in Kansas because of day-to-day discrimination on the basis of her ethnicity and language in schools that discouraged Spanish and did not recognize Latinx culture. For example, Patricia speaks English with a Dominican Spanish accent. As the lead teacher in her own classroom, some visitors often stereotyped Patricia as less capable because of language biases, addressing the assistant teacher, who was African American, with questions, instead of her. Growing up, because of messages sent by the colonized society in which she lived, Patricia hated her kinky-curly hair and she wanted hair like the White people she saw on television and in books. Her primary support came, not from schooling, but from family, with her grandmother often reassuring her: "Don't worry, because one day White people are gonna want hair like yours. You are lucky 'cause you can do your hair in so many ways!" These kinds of experiences drove Patricia's excitement for the PDCRT project, because it gave her an opportunity to learn how to be an even better bilingual teacher so that the children she teaches will be confident in who they are and the language they speak.

Kindel

Kindel Turner Nash, who self-identifies as a White woman connected to the African American community by marriage and family, was an assistant professor of Language & Literacy at the University of Missouri, Kansas City during her time as a PDCRT dyad and is now an associate professor of Early Childhood Education at the University of Maryland, Baltimore County. She grew up mainly in rural parts of South Carolina.

Like Patricia, Kindel is invested in culturally sustaining and asset-based teaching because of significant personal experiences as the mother and wife of people of Color and a former early childhood teacher in urban schools. For example, recently, she and her husband were awakened in the middle of the night by gunshots from their next-door neighbor's yard. Her husband, who is Black, called the police and they promptly arrived, but when her husband stepped out of the

FIGURE 2.2 Kindel Turner Nash.

front door of their house to speak to them, the cops told him to put his hands up, and pulled their guns out—treating him like a criminal on his own front porch. Furthermore, as a young, White teacher of culturally and linguistically diverse students, Kindel often faced challenges, struggling initially with "managing" her classroom, mostly because her preservice program had not equipped her to move beyond her own cultural and racial understandings to support children from racial and ethnic backgrounds different from her own (Nash, 2013). These complex and continuous incidents and facets of identity have led her to focus her research and teaching on justice-oriented practices in culturally, racially, and linguistically diverse classrooms. A former graduate student of Kindel's, Theresa, who had worked closely with Patricia in Head Start programs for many years, introduced us. Immediately, Patricia and Kindel felt that they had much to learn from each other.

As Kindel spent time each week in Patricia's classroom, observing the gentle way that she talked across languages, instructed, learned with, played with, and disciplined the children at El Centro, Kindel knew that she was witnessing not just culturally relevant but culturally sustaining pedagogies that critically centered "multicultural, multilingual, and justice pedagogies" (Kinloch, 2017, p. 39) in and beyond the students' school lives. These were pedagogies that forefronted the language and heritage practices of El Centro's community by recognizing "language as a crucial form of sustenance in its own right" and leveraging cultural practices as "resources both for achieving institutional access and for challenging structural inequality" (Bucholtz, Casillas, & Lee, 2017, pp. 44–45).

El Centro Academy

El Centro Academy for Children (El Centro Inc., n.d.) is a small dual-language and community partnership preschool which works to advance the significance and interconnectedness of children's heritage language, identities, and learning (Nash & Sosinski, 2015). Nestled in a small enclave that is adjacent to a large metropolitan Midwestern city that is home to a population of which about 55% are Latinx immigrants, 70% of El Centro's students are Latinx emergent bilinguals (El Centro Inc., n.d.; United States Census, 2010). El Centro is seen as the go-to place for local granting agencies and early childhood researchers because of the interdependent nature of not-for-profit groups, schools, and organizations working with the Latinx community in this region. El Centro has partnerships with the local school district and several universities including the one Kindel worked for at the time (University of Missouri, Kansas City). Theresa Torres, a longtime advocate for Latinx people in the Kansas City region and professor of Latinx studies at the University of Missouri, Kansas City, calls El Centro "a Latinx serving organization with a longstanding history of leadership and advocacy for Latinx in this region" (Torres, n.d.). El Centro's five classrooms each have two teachers: one speaks Spanish as their heritage language, the other English. During our work together, Patricia was the designated native Spanish-speaking teacher in her classroom of three-/four-year-olds.

Housed in a recently renovated Catholic School, El Centro is part of a local non-profit organization with a mission "to strengthen communities and improve lives of Latinos and others through educational, social, and economic opportunities" (El Centro Inc., n.d.). El Centro's mission is systematically enacted through its dual-language curriculum, teaching, evaluation, and hiring practices (Nash & Sosinski, 2015). While dual-language approaches are often rooted in binary delivery models that promote language separation (Palmer & Martínez, 2016), the approach at El Centro centers around viewing children's, parents', teachers', and families' language identities from an assets standpoint, where languages are seen as "multiple … and embodied in their everyday linguistic and pedagogical practices" (Martínez, Hikida, & Durán, 2015, p. 27). Patricia incorporated these multiple and embodied language practices into all aspects of the 8:00 a.m–5:00 p.m. day, which included the following daily routine: breakfast, circle time, small group, center time, gross-motor play, quiet time, lunch, rest, snack, read-aloud, center, clean-up, and more gross-motor play.

Patricia was a leavening force in her classroom and school—her presence brought equilibrium and stability to the students, families, and other adults. She was clearly an inspiration to many around her at El Centro, shining her light on others and making children, colleagues, and families feel welcomed and appreciated. Other teachers would often pop their heads into Patricia's room to smile and greet Patricia and her students. Patricia found that teachers throughout her building seemed eager to learn about translanguaging and our work to create culturally sustaining curriculum, which eventually led to a school-wide professional development on anti-bias teaching practices. Family members of current and past students also readily came to her classroom to stop to chat. However, there were other visitors to Patricia's classroom who did not seem to fold into its warmth in the same way. People from the various El Centro partnerships such as the local school district often came into Patricia's classroom, yet they brought with them a tension that Patricia said both she and the children felt. As Patricia explained, their purpose was solely to give tests to the children and tell her what she should be doing without attempting to understand anything about her children or their families. Within this school and classroom context Patricia and Kindel co-investigated and curricularized many culturally sustaining early literacy practices.

Organizing Our Research Work Together

Kindel spent one full day per week for an academic year in Patricia's classroom. Starting from day one of our work together, we cultivated a relationship and established strategies for communicating with each other as we collected and thought about classroom data together. These included weekly naptime conversations and text messages written back-and-forth to share photos and other insights throughout the week. Even so, the power hierarchy often perceived between university and teachers often became visible. One way it took form was in the way Patricia told everyone that Kindel was "a very smart person from the university." For this reason, Kindel tried to actively decenter her university role when she came to Patricia's classroom. She did this by taking on similar roles as Patricia such as being called Ms. Kindel instead of Dr. Nash, serving lunch to the children alongside Patricia, tucking children in at naptime, playing on the floor with the children, and reading aloud during circle time. Other ways that we tried to cultivate our partnership involved:

- reading professional books together during weekly hour-long sessions;
- sharing photos and stories of our lives;
- collaborating to plan lessons;
- engaging in discussion about teaching during naptime;
- getting together socially outside of school.

Understanding Culturally Sustaining Concepts through Patricia's Teaching

Patricia built her teaching on three tenets of culturally relevant pedagogy as Gloria Ladson-Billings (1995) has outlined: building students' cultural competence, critical consciousness, and academic achievement. However, over time we came to embrace the specificity of culturally sustaining pedagogy (CSP) (Paris & Alim, 2017) as an ideology that centers curriculum around community languages, practices, and knowledge; ensures student agency and community input; connects learning to "histories of racial, ethnic, and linguistic communities" (Paris & Alim, 2017, n.p.); and develops students' capacity to address oppression while working to sustain such teaching as the pedagogical norm. CSP's focus on multilingualism and linguistic dexterity perfectly describes Patricia's translanguaging practices, which sought to "foster-to sustain-linguistic … and cultural dexterity" (Alim & Paris, 2017, p. 1). Such a focus was important because, while early childhood language and literacy development is often portrayed as a line of regression, or a lockstep set of stage-by-stage milestones, with Yaden (2013) we came to see emergent bi/multilingual children's learning in Patricia's classroom as better represented by a *hyperbolic plane* (Figure 2.3). This ecological view of early literacy and language learning positions "the development of children and adults as situated within and across the demands of participation in the multiple routine sites of activity in which people are engaged," seeing these intersecting sites as "dynamically interacting" (Lee, 2017, pp. 261–262).

Geometrically, a hyperbolic plane is the opposite of a sphere:

> On a sphere, the surface curves in on itself and is closed, [while] a hyperbolic plane is a surface in which the space curves away from itself at every point … it is open and infinite [with] a more complex and counterintuitive geometry. (Wertheim, 2005, n.p.)

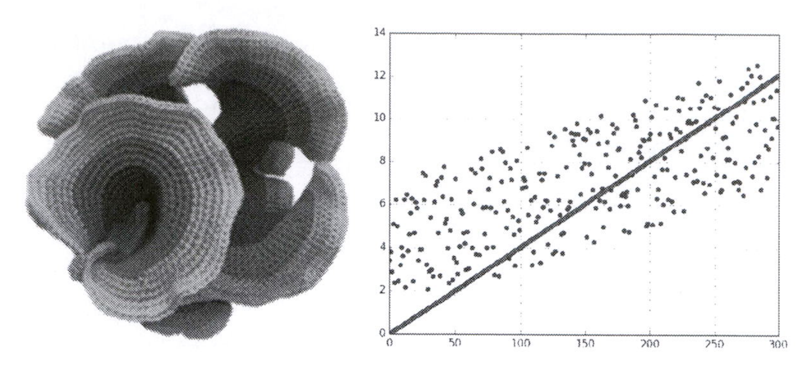

FIGURE 2.3 Children's learning as a hyperbolic plane in contrast to a line of regression. Photos licensed under CC BY-SA-NC (left) and CC BY-SA (right).

We feel the hyperbolic plane represents the sociocultural, ecological nature of children's learning in Patricia's preschool classroom and helps us capture ways that her everyday teaching practices were complex, contextualized, and multifaceted. In particular, we focus on three practices which pivot on Patricia's translanguaging (Garza & Langman, 2014). These practices include specific culturally sustaining, in-the-moment translanguaging practices and curriculum, warm-demanding teaching (Bondy & Ross, 2008; Gay, 2010) through *consejos*, and early literacy assessment (Piña, Nash, Boardman, Polson, & Panther, 2015). Translanguaging was originally defined as "the planned and systematic use of two languages for teaching and learning inside the same lesson" (Williams, 1994, n.p.). García (2009) revived the term to showcase the complex, dynamic, and flexible ways in which bilingual people mesh languages and codes employing a rich repertoire of fluid linguistic turns when speaking along a "continua of biliteracy" (Hornberger & Link, 2012, p. 240). Translanguaging is different from previous thinking about bilingualism because it does not see a bilingual's language repertoire as made up of two distinct and separate languages that are linearly and separately acquired and used: bilingual people are not two monolinguals in one, and bilingualism is not simply the sum of one language and the other. Ofelia García speaks of dynamic bilingualism in describing the complex language practices of bilinguals, shedding the notion of additive bilingualism, and recognizing translanguaging as a bilingual discursive norm (Celic & Seltzer, 2013, p. 3).

We emphasize translanguaging in our discussion of classroom examples, directly connecting it with key features of culturally sustaining pedagogies, including: (a) a critical centering on languages, practices, and ways of knowing that (b) extend from and are accountable to children, families, and their communities, through (c) historicized instruction while (d) fostering children's understanding and ability to confront oppressive and colonizing messages (Paris & Alim, 2017).

In-the-Moment Translanguaging Practices and Curriculum in Patricia's Classroom

Patricia employed translanguaging in skillful ways, demonstrating a commitment to sustaining children's identities and languages (Paris & Alim, 2017). Patricia's critical centering of languages happened in the moment, as she made decisions based on the child and the context. As she said:

> I don't just talk to them in just one language. I teach them in both Spanish and English, so I can make sure they understand me. If I say something in English and the child doesn't understand, then I say it in Spanish.

An example of this organic, in-the-moment language centering happened every day at naptime, when Javier, a young boy in Patricia's class, would say, "Ms., Ms., will you wrap me up '¿como un burrito?" to which Patricia would playfully and joyfully reply, "'¿Como un burrito?' You want me to wrap you like that?" "Yes, yes!" he would exclaim, giggling happily (Piña et al., 2015, p. 13). This repeated translanguaging practice helped foster Javier's safety and comfort at naptime, a difficult time for him. In this way, Patricia normalized the complex but intuitive practice of translanguaging across Spanish and English to honor and encourage his fluid use of both languages. In doing so, she critically centered and validated his ability to speak two languages and recognized the cognitive triumph that he exhibited in being able to manipulate two languages to communicate what neither language could express on its own. In this way she held herself accountable to the community she was teaching through meaningfully foregrounding perhaps the most important aspect of children's selves and communities—their language (Paris & Alim, 2017). Through these on-the-spot decisions to translanguage, Patricia also helped children and families confront colonizing English-only discourses.

Helping Children and Families Confront and Counter English-Only Discourses and Policies

The normalization of translanguaging through Patricia's everyday decisions to talk across languages in the classroom proved very important to all children in her class as they gained fluency in both languages and used them as needed. However, some families objected to the co-mingling of languages, concerned that their children would not gain English fluency if given license to weave Spanish into and out of their utterances. It is likely that this attitude is the result of the influence of English-only discourses and policies prevalent in societal and educational contexts that constantly send messages that "children and families are the problem, that they are lacking in rich languages, cultures, and histories" (Paris & Alim, 2017). As a result of these messages, families often "internalize false understandings of ourselves, our practices, our communities, and our futures"

(Paris & Alim, 2017), trusting those who espouse such ideas because they typically represent authority structures in educational institutions (Dyson, 2015; García, 2009). Patricia also saw English-only policies as an assault on families' and children's identities, knowing from professional experience and irrefutable evidence from language research that children learn new languages with greater efficiency when they use their heritage/home languages fluidly and freely (Canagarajah, 2011; Genishi & Dyson, 2009; Rosa & Flores, 2017).

This knowledge and expertise in supporting children's dynamic translanguaging practices led Patricia to confront—and encourage children and family members to confront and counter—negative and colonizing English-only discourses. She did so by sharing her knowledge of the importance of using both languages and moving in and out of them as necessary. For example, three-year-old Josué's mother came to pick up her son and heard Patricia speaking to him in a hybrid form of Spanish and English. Using both languages herself, Josué's mother told Patricia, "No español, no español, es muy importante que Josué hable inglés, No Spanish, No Spanish!" Patricia challenged the mother across languages, saying, "No es un buena idea, because if children can speak in English and Spanish they are learning both languages, and they are smarter than other kids." In this exchange, Patricia employed translanguaging practices in order to explain the importance of translanguaging to the parent: she demonstrated the power of utilizing two languages by explaining and using both languages in her explanation. Patricia challenged, and at the same time gave Josué's mother the tools to confront the prevalent colonizing message of English-only discourse.

For Patricia, another vital way of confronting and countering English-only discourses through translanguaging involved teaching children to appreciate and utilize (and demand that others do so too) the Spanish pronunciation of their names. Enactment of this strategy arose from Patricia's strong conviction about the importance of authentic name pronunciation, recognizing that names are reflections of our cultural and linguistic histories and inherent parts of our identities. She was adamant that if a child was named Juliana, Sebastian, José, or Isabella, the names should never be Anglicized to Joo-lee-an-na, Ce-bass-tee-en, Jos-say, or Iz-a-bell. Putting this belief into action, one day, a testing administrator from the local school district came to Patricia's class, asking to give an assessment to "Ce-bass-tien." Patricia looked the testing administrator in the eye and pronounced his name correctly, "Ah, Sebastian?" (Sa-bas-tee-un). She then turned to Sebastian, who was seated on the rug and called: "Sebastian, Vénte aquí, esta maestra has something for you to do." Pronouncing his name correctly, she set an example for the visitor while validating the child's heritage language and communicating with him in their familiar way. Not only did she insist that others pronounce her students' names correctly, she also demanded that the children pronounce their *own* names correctly. For example, in an everyday conversation with a child from her class, Julia, Patricia repeatedly reinforced this idea through a playful interaction (Piña et al., 2015):

PATRICIA: Te llamas JULIA [Anglicized pronunciation of /J/]/Is your name JULIA?
JULIA: Noooooo, mi nombre es JULIA [Spanish pronunciation of /J/]

Patricia went on to scaffold Julia's ability to correct potential mispronunciations of her name:

PATRICIA: And if some calls you Goo-lia? [Anglicized pronunciation of /J/] What do you say?
JULIA: Me llama es JULIA! [Spanish pronunciation of /J/]

Patricia also involved Julia's mother in this interaction, emphasizing to her that she must never let anyone mispronounce Julia's name. She extended her belief about the importance of names to practices such as: making bilingual class books featuring children's names, including children's names with accents on the alphabet chart and on other labels, and many other practices (Figure 2.4 shows an example of a class Name Book—for a complete list of strategies see Table 1 in Piña et al., 2015, p. 10).

Nuestras Nombres

Our Names

FIGURE 2.4 Nuestros Nombres/Our Names, a class Name Book.

Valuing the cultural wealth represented in a name, Patricia worked to help children and their families confront widespread negative messaging about the pronunciation and writing of their names while forefronting children's and families' communities and "their practices beyond the dominant narratives of White, middle class, 'standard' English monolingual/monocultural superiority which schools largely uphold" (Paris & Alim, 2017).

Songs, Books, and Labeling the Room

Patricia created multilingual curriculum through song, books, and classroom labels to critically center the cultural dexterity of children and families' languaging practices. For example, Patricia and her class sang a particular song each day during morning circle time in exactly this way:

> ¿Hola, como estas, hola, coma estas, como estas this morning?
> ¿Hola, como estas, hola, coma estas, como estas this morning?
> ¿Hola, como estas, hola, coma estas, como estas this morning?

After singing the song as a class, each child would then greet the child beside them in the circle, shaking hands and saying "*¿Hola, como estas?*" The familiar routine of singing this greeting song was a daily affirmation of the importance of talking across multiple languages.

Similarly, Patricia went out of her way to create bilingual pattern books that were authored by and featured photos of children. One such text, entitled *¡Yo, si puedo!/ Yes, I Can!* was created by the students as Patricia encouraged translanguaging through discussion about daily classroom engagements they each enjoyed (e.g., gross-motor play in the gym or on the playground, the book center, tricycle riding, blocks, etc.). After much daily talking, writing, and photography about things they can do, each child created an Yo, si puedo/Yes, I can page of the class book (Figure 2.5) by writing and/or drawing a word to complete the sentence stem Yo, si puedo/ Yes, I can ______. This book was placed in the Lectura/Reading Area where children would often choose to read this text over the other books available there. Singing songs and writing class books across multiple languages was a powerful experience for many of the children as it foregrounded and fostered their dexterous language and community knowledge (Paris & Alim, 2017) while giving them ownership over writing and teaching them multilingual sentence patterns which they could read and rehearse every day (Laman, 2013).

In addition to creating class songs and books, Patricia used translanguaging techniques to label classroom projects and areas throughout the room so that Spanish was privileged over English (a school-wide practice) (Figure 2.6). Patricia's labels were in Spanish and English, but teachers should be encouraged to create (and create with children) labels that reflect all the languages represented in their classroom. Like the songs and books, multilingual labeling is culturally

Yo Si Puedo
Yes I Can

FIGURE 2.5 Yo si puedo/Yes I can! A Spanish/English class book.

sustaining as it foregrounds children's heritage language. Multilingual labeling is also important to multilingual language development since it fosters children's connections between their heritage languages and English while simultaneously building receptive vocabulary (Laman, 2013).

In addition to the labels on areas and objects in the classroom, at the beginning of the year, each child/family in Patricia's class put together a poster collage of family photos. Patricia then labeled each poster ¡Mi Familia My Family! and posted them along the wall so that these were one of the first things people see when entering the room.

FIGURE 2.6 Translanguaging labels on classroom projects.

The strategies described to this point comprised what we see now to be culturally sustaining translanguaging practices in Patricia's class—reassuring families and helping them confront colonizing English-only discourses, valuing names, and creating curriculum that normalizes children's and families' heritage language through classroom songs, books, and labels. Supporting heritage practices and language through translanguaging along with fluidly and seamlessly but intentionally developing students' abilities with the language of power actually promotes the development of new language expertise (Dyson, 2013; García, 2009; Genishi & Goodwin, 2008; Gort & Sembiante, 2015). Table 2.1 offers additional examples of in-the-moment translanguaging strategies that teachers of students who speak multiple languages can use. The next section describes Patricia's translanguaging through warm-demanding *consejos*.

Translanguaging and Warm-Demanding Consejos

Patricia was a warm demander. The term *warm demander* was first used to describe the approach taken by teachers of Athabaskan Indian students in Alaskan school settings (Kleinfeld, 1975). Kleinfeld described these teachers as exhibiting both "personal warmth" and "active demandingness" (pp. 326–327). While much of the research

TABLE 2.1 In-the-moment translanguaging in the culturally sustaining early literacy classroom.

Translanguaging strategy	*Description*
Utilizing hybrid verbs/heteroglossic words (Garza & Langman, 2014, p. 44)	Teachers/students conversationally use hybrid words like "pushear" (to push)—an English verb with a Spanish suffix.
Content/correction in both languages (Garza & Langman, 2014, p. 44)	Teacher identifies students' mistakes in non-threatening ways and defines terms in both languages.
Emphasis on the task instead of the language (Garza & Langman, 2014, p. 42)	Teacher acknowledges, honors, and validates the student's choice to use either language at any time.
Language meshing (Martínez, Hikida, & Durán, 2015, p. 38)	Teacher switches back and forth or meshes the language of instruction and heritage language.
Incorporating and playing with dialectical language features (Martínez, Hikida, & Durán, 2015, p. 37)	Teacher uses syntactic features of multiple heritage language dialects (e.g., intentionally using the Salvadoran dialect or selecting children's books to make a new student from El Salvador feel more comfortable).
Language meshing during literacy engagements; includes recontextualization, voice strategies, interactional strategies, and textualization strategies (Canagarajah, 2011; Smith & Murillo, 2015, p. 62)	Teacher models both speaking and writing in multiple languages using description, tone, verbal and non-verbal cues (see below).
• Recontextualization	Teacher gauges the reader's ability to comprehend and appreciate instances of code-meshing during a read-aloud.
• Voice strategies	Using code-meshing to articulate the author's voice rather than convey meaning.
• Interactional strategies	Actively negotiating and co-constructing meaning with the reader to avoid miscommunication while interacting with a read-aloud.
• Textualization strategies	Attempting to convey sensory perceptions and emotion rather than meaning.

on warm-demanding teaching has focused on teachers of African American students (Bondy & Ross, 2008; Delpit, 2012; Gay, 2010; Irvine & Fraser, 1998; Ware, 2006), Volk's (2013) ethnography of Latinx families' home and community literacies identified Latinx parents' child-rearing practices as warm-demanding. Latinx parents in Volk's study described family members who demanded with warmth as they asserted high-expectations and supported children in meeting those expectations. They were also warm demanders as they provided life advice and built caring relationships by sharing *consejos*—teachings in the form of brief stories that built on their own life experiences and struggles—to inspire their children's success (Volk, 2015, p. 14).

Like the warm demanders in Volk's (2013) ethnography, Patricia skillfully used *consejos*, meshing Spanish and English together to assert her expectations for students. For example, one morning, the children were seated on the large colorful carpet in the circle time area where Patricia, also seated in the circle, had just finished reading the picture book *Colores/Colors* by Eric Carle (2008). She was explaining the upcoming engagement, a science experiment using food color and paper towels, when a student, Guillermo, began to talk over Patricia, distracting other children. Patricia then used a *consejo* to illustrate her expectation that Guillermo needed to be listening to her explanation. First, she moved into a chair just outside the circle and pulled Guillermo on her lap. She spoke directly to him and then to the entire class, crossing back and forth between English and Spanish:

PATRICIA: Guillermo, did you know that if we all talk at the same time we cannot understand each other? You jus gonna hear that (using her hand to demonstrate a talking mouth). You gonna hear, *Ra-ra-ra-ra-ra*. Do you understand why I say that?

GUILLERMO: (shakes head yes)

PATRICIA: When my son was in school, he sometimes forgot to listen to his teacher. But then, he didn't know what to do. So next time, pay attention, *escúchame* (taps her head with finger,) *listen* to what the maestra is telling you because it can be something very important. Okay? Now go to your carpet, please.

GUILLERMO: (walks rejoin circle by sitting on his carpet spot)

PATRICIA: (to the entire class) Did you know we were talking at the same time? (class looks at Patricia, some nod). If I say ra-ra-ra-ra-ra, what did I say? (to Guillermo) You can't hear what I'm saying, because if we talk at the same time—Try to talk, and I'm going to try to talk, too. Say something, Guillermo. *Di algo, Guillermo.*

GUILLERMO: (talks softly)

PATRICIA: (at the same time) Da, da, da, da, da. [to class] You don't know what I'm talking about, do you?

This is one illustration of Patricia's everyday warm-demanding teaching and her particular use of a Spanish/English *consejo* about her son to communicate her expectations. We see these warm-demanding practices as culturally sustaining because of their alignment to some of the historicized parenting practices used in the children's homes, while standing in contrast to prevalent policies and practices in many early childhood classrooms which draw from White, middle-class standards of parenting and teaching (Paris & Alim, 2017). For instance, a commonly used technique when children distract others from the focus of the lesson is to "redirect" or "offer choices" (Gartrell, 2013, p. 239), typically suggested as a universalistic, one-size-fits-all approach to child guidance. Yet, to address the issue in a culturally sustaining way, Patricia historicized her curricula through sustaining the heritage practice (Paris & Alim, 2014,) of the *consejo*, simultaneously translanguaging to reflect the interwoven use of multiple languages (Paris & Alim, 2017). In this way, she reflected understandings of Latinx culture and language as "dynamic, shifting, and encompassing both past-oriented heritage dimensions and present-oriented community dimensions" (Paris & Alim, 2014, p. 90) while critically centering on children and their families.

Translanguaging in Assessment Practices

In much the same way that Patricia translanguaged through in-the-moment practices and warm-demanding *consejos* to critically center children's and families linguistic and cultural dexterity and confront colonizing messages about their language, she also used translanguaging practices to comprehensively assess children's language and literacy knowledge. She administered assessments by meshing languages, developed multiple forms of authentic, Spanish–English assessments, and set particular goals for each student. She assessed those goals in numerous ways which she found useful and important for planning and sharing information with parents—through anecdotal notes, observation checklists, formative assessments, informal conversations with children, and photos/samples of student work, all maintained in a bound portfolio for each child in her class. While all of these assessment strategies have been shown to be highly effective for authentic assessment in multilingual, early childhood classroom settings (Genishi & Dyson, 2009; Piña et al., 2015), oftentimes, Patricia's culturally sustaining and comprehensive portfolios were disregarded with respect to external evaluations of her students' kindergarten readiness. Instead of looking at the detailed records she kept, many students in her class were assessed by an external evaluator from the school district, who used English-only summative assessments such as the Peabody Picture Vocabulary Test (PPVT-III) and the Developmental Indicators for the Assessment of Learning (DIAL-IV). Patricia lamented the fact that often, these summative assessments needed to be administered in the child's home language, explaining that when they were not, too many children get sent to special education—kids who did not need to be in special education. Patricia worried constantly about the fact that children learning a new language might be seen as unintelligent and have to go to a special class. Patricia wanted for her children the same thing she wanted for her own son, also a second language learner—an education that did not conflate his language learning with a disability.

Patricia's intuition that students were being over-referred for special education as a result of language and not disability is true. Both the PPVT-III and the DIAL-IV have been shown to be biased in terms of culture, language, and content (Laing & Kamhi, 2003). In fact, research has shown that tests such as these may contribute to disproportionate numbers of Latinx students being identified for special education for language and learning disabilities (Fletcher & Navarrete, 2011; Irizarry, 2017; Skiba et al., 2008).

Patricia's fear was realized in early spring when one of her newest students, Santiago, was referred for special education as a result of his performance on the DIAL-IV. Santiago was one of the youngest four-year-olds in the class, which he had only recently joined early in February, moving there three months before his fourth birthday, because school personnel agreed Patricia could "handle him better." Santiago was not talking at all when he came into Patricia's class. He often whacked over items as he barreled from one activity center to the next, yet Santiago did not seem angry or overly emotional. While his behaviors were of concern to El Centro's administrator (this is the reason she moved him to Patricia's class), Patricia and Kindel noted that he had a very affectionate nature and did not exhibit aggressive behavior toward other children. By early March, Santiago had begun to communicate in both Spanish and English. Patricia told Kindel that she noticed that he seemed to struggle with pronunciation of Spanish and English phonemes, but she knew that this was typical among children his age (Genishi & Dyson, 2009). Yet soon after he came to Patricia's class, Santiago was flagged for special education testing by local school district personnel purportedly because of his hesitancy to speak in English or Spanish in school. One day in mid-March, Kindel arrived at Patricia's classroom to find Patricia very upset. Santiago had just failed the language articulation portion of the DIAL-IV assessment, which had been administered only in English by a testing administrator, a stranger to Santiago, who was a special education coordinator for the local school district. As the children in her class played, Patricia explained Santiago's testing encounter:

KINDEL: So the special education teacher came?

PATRICIA: Yes, and you know, they [the children] don't feel comfortable sometimes with the strangers. So, so he got zero on the language part of test [the part that orally assesses first/last name, age, day, month year as well as phonemic awareness]. I told the lady that he might need Speech, but he should not have failed, he definitely knew his name and age and he could say most of his letters. I tried to show them his portfolio.

KINDEL: So did they not take your assessments in account at all?

PATRICIA: No, they do their own assessments.

Patricia showed Kindel the DIAL-IV testing document that Santiago had been administered, which she had been given for her records. Patricia said she felt Santiago failed because he was confused and intimidated, being tested in English (a language he was in the process of acquiring) and having never met the testing administrator before. Two of the items he "failed" were saying his first name and identifying the letter "S" as the first letter of his name. This was frustrating to Patricia as she had seen him say his name and identify the "S" regularly. She called Santiago over to where we were sitting:

PATRICIA: Can you go get your journal, Santiago?
SANTIAGO: (Walks to writing center and picks up his journal out of a basket with many others. His first name was in typed print on the front of the journal).
PATRICIA: Can you write your letter "S" please.
SANTIAGO: (Opens journal, writes letter "S").
PATRICIA: Look at the [alphabet] chart. *¿Dónde está* letter S?
SANTIAGO: (Looks at alphabet chart, then points to S in his name on his journal).
PATRICIA: Yes, S is for Santiago. S is for *el sapo*. S is for *salchichas*.

In contrast to his performance on the English-only assessment, this authentic and contextualized, translanguaged assessment showcased his actual understandings: Santiago *did* recognize his first name. He *did* know the letter "S." He did understand the concept of a letter and he could identify letters on the class alphabet chart. He was able to transfer that letter knowledge to identifying a letter in his own name.

Evidenced the example above, Patricia put her strong beliefs about the value of her children's community practices and language knowledge into action as she enacted sustaining assessment practices that were linked to and accountable to her students and their families (Paris & Alim, 2017). Traditional assessments, on the other hand, represent and were constructed to mark children of Color as deficient rather than asking how schools might sustain "the lifeways of communities who have been and continue to be damaged and erased through schooling" (Alim & Paris, 2017, p. 1). Even so, Patricia did help her students meet "grade level objectives" such traditional assessments measured. According to Patricia and El Centro's director, Geralyn Sosinski, Patricia's students met or exceeded the learning targets for three- and four-year-olds each year. This success may very well be attributable to her use of authentic, contextualized, translanguaged assessments. Table 2.2 includes culturally sustaining early childhood assessment practices that Patricia used to authentically assess her three-/four-year-olds' literacy and language.

The Power of the Dyad Relationship

Our dyad relationship was light-hearted as well as very serious in nature, characterized by warmth, love, and respect. For example, Kindel could not find a good hairstylist and Patricia insisted that she allow her aunt, a professional hairstylist, to cut her hair at their kitchen table. Strategies that fostered our relationship included:

- treating each other with respect, love, and generosity;
- spending time together outside of the school context;
- Kindel actively decentering her academic role and status;

TABLE 2.2 Culturally sustaining early literacy assessment strategies.

Assessment/Strategy	*Target Area*	*Application in Patricia's class*
Informal Book Handling and Print Awareness Assessment	Book Handling and Print and Picture Awareness through Multilingual Children's Literature	Patricia observes how children interact with culturally authentic, multilingual books throughout the day.
Contextualized Letter Assessment	Letter Identification and Awareness	Patricia pre-makes a set of alphabet letters (uppercase and lowercase) on index cards and hangs an alphabet wall with children and families' names, and pictures from the school and community environmental print. Each morning during centers, she asks students to match the pre-made letter cards with the letters on the wall.
Letter Sorts	Letter Identification and Awareness	Patricia provides an English and Spanish set of pre-made letters and a whiteboard or other surface and scaffolds children to sort letters (by color, shape, and attributes, name, etc.) during small group time.
Record of Oral Language across Languages	Oral Language & Syntax	A child repeats a sentence (sentences become increasingly complex) spoken by Patricia—in one or more languages throughout the day.
Multilingual Tell Me a Story	Multilingual Oral Narrative Production	Patricia reads the child a text across languages and asks children to retell the text to another child across languages.

- maintaining clear communication through text messages, instant messaging, and phone calls; and
- meeting every week at a designated time that worked for both of us (like naptime).

Challenges ranged from our mutual dislike and feelings of powerlessness because of predominant English-only policies in the feeder district, and the seemingly omnipresent district testing administrators, to lack of time to read and study culturally relevant and sustaining teaching together, and difficulty finding time to create the new materials needed to center children's languages and communities beyond the resources available at El Centro.

Yet, our work to generate and better understand culturally relevant pedagogies in that first year proved more complex, challenging, and heavy than we expected and the strength of our friendship was revealed in a variety of ways. When Kindel's oldest daughter was hospitalized in the spring of that year, Patricia became a true friend, often chatting with and meeting with Kindel after school and sharing love, encouragement, and support. A few months later at the end of our first year working together, Patricia announced that she would be leaving her job at El Centro and was considering leaving teaching altogether. Continued tensions, reinforced year after year when children like Santiago were referred to special education despite her wishes and her knowledge about their capacity, were degrading and demoralizing experiences for her. These experiences made her emotionally sick and, ultimately made her declare, "I just can't take it anymore." Patricia's leaving the school because of frustration with unjust practices and policies reflects larger trends of teachers of Color leaving teaching, not because they are burned out, but because they cannot stand to witness the continued degradation of children (Sutcher, Darling-Hammond, & Carter-Thomas, 2016). Even so, Patricia's decision to leave helped us articulate the complexities of teaching and the criticality of culturally relevant teaching and, as we write this piece, culturally sustaining pedagogies as a necessary response to those complexities. Patricia and Kindel remained in contact throughout the second year of the project, and remain committed to this work and to telling the stories of success and of injustice that we uncovered through our partnership in the PDCRT project as we work together to discuss and disseminate this research.

We Must Keep Working

This chapter has described a few of the translanguaging practices utilized in Patricia's multilingual classroom at El Centro Academy as well as our dyad relationship. We see our relationship and these practices as clear examples of the very complex, every day, moment-to-moment, connections and actions that demand outcomes centered around the richness of multiple languages and multiple heritage and community practices. While we began with a culturally relevant approach, we see these practices as culturally sustaining because Patricia was intentional in her use of them to "resist static, unidirectional notions of culture" (Paris & Alim, 2014, p. 95) by nurturing and actively promoting the linguistic dexterity of her students and families—concurrently *sustaining* cultural and linguistic knowledge and *developing* expertise in the language of power (Dyson, 2013; Paris, 2012).

The examples in this chapter also illustrate the *hyperbolic nature* of early language and literacy learning as sociocultural, ecological, complex, contextualized, and multifaceted processes. When children's language and literacy learning is represented by a dexterous figure like the hyperbolic plane (Figure 2.1), we can begin to visualize the breathtaking sociolinguistic diversity of children's language and literacy development (Genishi & Dyson, 2009). As Patricia demonstrated, and a wealth of research into learning and language affirms, this means that children:

- *Do not* develop and learn on step by step, yearlong timelines but rather learn everything multiple times, both internally and in social spaces (Bruner & Haste, 2010; Clay, 1985; Clay, Gill, Glynn, McNaughton, & Salmon, 2007; Lee, 2017; Vygotsky, 1978).

- *Do* learn in ecologically mediated, socially constructed activities through using languages which help them give meaning—to regulate, negotiate, and express relationships between themselves and in connection with their learning (Lee, 2017; Genishi & Dyson, 2009).

In this chapter, we also provided examples of tools that early childhood educators can use to navigate multidimensional linguistic classrooms, whether they are monolingual or multilingual themselves. In sum, these tools include:

- enacting in-the-moment decisions to translanguage;
- making translanguaged class books featuring children's names;
- singing translanguaged songs;
- creating pattern books written across languages;
- labeling the room/class projects so that Spanish (and other languages) are privileged over English;
- meshing multiple languages throughout talk and teaching;
- telling translanguaged warm-demanding *consejos* to communicate complex, abstract ideas;
- meshing multiple languages to authentically assess children's language and literacy learning and development.

With others (Dyson, 2013; Genishi & Dyson, 2009; Laman, 2013; Souto-Manning & Martell, 2016) we encourage readers to carefully rethink the preschool language and literacy practices and assessments such as English-only assessments or rigid linear expectations requiring progression from one milestone to the next (for example, speaking Spanish one day/English the next, learning a letter of the week, or mastering all letters before moving onto letter–sound relationships). We know that these assessments and lockstep expectations are based on a myth of homogenous, White, middle-class norms that neglect, suppress, and pathologize minoritized children's heritage and community languages and literacies (Irizarry, 2017; Lee, 2017). Within such deficit frameworks, children's full range of expertise and knowledge is ignored, leading to lifelong feelings of inadequacy (Long et al., 2013; Paris & Alim, 2014, 2017). In contrast, classrooms that value, utilize, and promote translanguaging in the context of language and literacy instruction lead not only to expertise in two or more languages, but confidence that supports further learning, greater cognitive abilities than are present in English-only brains, and preparation for insightful interaction in a global society. The need for culturally sustaining pedagogies in schools, which are microcosms of society, is clear. Discrimination against emerging bi/multilinguals is reflected around the country in and out of schools as young children and their families are told: "You're in America now, speak English," "You are gonna be sent back to Mexico," and "You don't belong here." Yet, an overwhelming amount of research tells us that emerging bi/multilingual children are many steps ahead of children who only speak English. Their social, global, linguistic, and cognitive skills reach far beyond those of their English-only peers (García, 2009; Genishi & Goodwin, 2008; Gort & Sembiante, 2015; Palmer, Martínez, Mateus, & Henderson, 2014). The two of us repeatedly discussed how these issues impacted us personally and professionally.

Finally, in the interest of sustaining these kinds of practices beyond Patricia's pre-K classroom or Kindel's teacher education courses, the challenge remains as to how to ensure that these practices do not merely represent a moment-in-time. This concern was, in fact, a reason why Patricia left El Centro. The dictates of the district requiring culturally and linguistically biased assessments and their refusal to listen to Patricia's pleas (year after year) to do otherwise reveal a lack of respect for the languages of her students and families and was frustrating at the very least. At the same time, we know that Patricia left a lasting impact on El Centro, sustaining change through normalizing the practice of translanguaging. After Patricia left, Kindel continued to teach education classes at the school, providing ongoing professional development on antiracist and asset-based pedagogies in work with families, teachers, and administrators. We feel, of course, that we could have done more. In our conversations, Patricia often reiterated her intention, her dream, expressed through her work for and with bi/multilingual children—"My dream is that one day there are not going to be any labels on the little ones. I know that feeling. That's why for us, we have no choice. We must keep working." And so, we must keep working.

References

Alim, H. S., & Paris, D. (2017). What is culturally sustaining pedagogy and why does it matter? In D. Paris & H. S. Alim (Eds.), *Culturally sustaining pedagogies: Teaching and learning for justice in a changing world.* (pp. 1–24). New York, NY: Teachers College Press.

Baines, J., Tisdale, C., & Long, S. (2018). *"We've been doing it your way long enough": Choosing the culturally relevant classroom.* New York, NY: Teachers College Press.

Bondy, E., & Ross, D. D. (2008). The teacher as warm demander. *The Positive Classroom*, 66, 54–58.

Bridwell, N. (2009). *Clifford the big red dog/Clifford el gran perro rojo.* New York, NY: Scholastic Press.

Bruner, J. S., & Haste, H. (Eds.). (2010). *Making sense: The child's construction of the world.* London: Routledge.

Bucholtz, M., Casillas, D. I., & Lee, J. S. (2017). Language and culture as sustenance. In D. Paris & H. S. Alim (Eds.), *Culturally sustaining pedagogies: Teaching and learning for justice in a changing world* (pp.43–59). New York, NY: Teachers College Press. Canagarajah, S. (2011). Translanguaging in the classroom: Emerging issues for research and pedagogy. *Applied Linguistics Review*, 2, 1–28.

Carle, E. (2008). *Colors/Colores.* New York, NY: Philomel Books.

Celic, C., & Seltzer, K. (2013). *Translanguaging: A CUNY-NYSIEB guide for educators.* New York, NY: CUNY-NYSIEB, The Graduate Center, The City University of New York.

Clay, M. M. (1985). *The early detection of reading difficulties.* Auckland: Heinemann.

Clay, M. M., Gill, M., Glynn, T., McNaughton, T., & Salmon, K. (2007). *Record of oral language: Observing changes in the acquisition of language structures*. Auckland: Heinemann.

Delpit, L. (2012). *"Multiplication is for White people": Raising expectations for other people's children*. New York, NY: The New Press.

Dyson, A. H. (2013). *Rewriting the basics: Literacy learning in children's cultures*. New York, NY: Teachers College Press.

Dyson, A. H. (2015). The search for inclusion: Deficit discourse and the erasure of childhoods. *Language Arts*, 92, 199–207.

El Centro, Inc. (n.d.). Retrieved from http://www.elcentroinc.com/

Fletcher, T. V., & Navarrete, L. A. (2011). Learning disabilities or difference: A critical look at issues associated with the misidentification and placement of Hispanic students in special education programs. *Rural Special Education Quarterly*, 30, 30–38.

García, O. (2009). *Bilingual education in the 21st century: A global perspective*. Malden, MA: Basil/Blackwell.

Gartrell, D. (2013). *A guidance approach for the encouraging classroom*. Belmont, CA: Wadsworth Cengage Learning.

Garza, A., & Langman, J. (2014). Translanguaging in a Latin@ bilingual community: Negotiations and mediations in a dual-language classroom. *Association of Mexican American Educators Journal*, 8, 37–49.

Gay, G. (2010). *Culturally responsive teaching: Theory, research, and practice*. New York, NY: Teachers College Press.

Genishi, C., & Dyson, A. H. (2009). *Children, language, and literacy: Diverse learners in diverse times*. New York, NY: Teachers College Press.

Genishi, C., & Goodwin, A. L. (2008). *Diversities in early childhood education: Rethinking and doing*. New York, NY: Routledge.

Gort, M., & Sembiante, S. F. (2015). Navigating hybridized language learning spaces through translanguaging pedagogy: Dual language preschool teachers' languaging practices in support of emergent bilingual children's performance of academic discourse. *International Multilingual Research Journal*, 9, 7–25.

Hollins, E. R. (2015). *Culture in school learning: Revealing the deep meaning*. London: Routledge.

Hornberger, N. H., & Link, H. (2012). Translanguaging and transnational literacies in multilingual classrooms: A biliteracy lens. *International Journal of Bilingual Education and Bilingualism*, 15, 227–261.

Irizarry, J. G. (2017). "For us, by us": A vision for culturally sustaining pedagogies forwarded by Latinx youth. In D. Paris & H. S. Alim (Eds.), *Culturally sustaining pedagogies: Teaching and learning for justice in a changing world* (pp. 83–98). New York, NY: Teachers College Press.

Irvine, J. J., & Fraser, J. W. (1998). Warm demanders. *Education Week, 17*(35), 56–57.

Kinloch, V. (2017). "You ain't making me write." In D. Paris & H. S. Alim (Eds.), *Culturally sustaining pedagogies: Teaching and learning for justice in a changing world* (pp. 25–43). New York, NY: Teachers College Press.

Kleinfeld, J. (1975). Effective teachers of Eskimo and Indian students. *The School Review*, 83, 301–344.

Ladson-Billings, G. (1995). Toward a theory of culturally relevant pedagogy. *American Educational Research Journal*, 32, 465–491.

Laing, S. P., & Kamhi, A. (2003). Alternative assessment of language and literacy in culturally and linguistically diverse populations. *Language, Speech, and Hearing Services in Schools*, 34, 44–55.

Laman, T. T. (2013). *From ideas to words: Writing strategies for English language learners*. Portsmouth, NH: Heinemann.

Lee, C. D. (2017). An ecological framework for enacting culturally sustaining pedagogy. In D. Paris & H. S. Alim (Eds.), *Culturally sustaining pedagogies: Teaching and learning for justice in a changing world* (pp. 261–274). New York, NY: Teachers College Press.

Long, S., Volk, D., Baines, J., & Tisdale, C. (2013). "We've been doing it your way long enough": Syncretism as a critical process. *Journal of Early Childhood Literacy*, 13, 418–439.

Martínez, R. A., Hikida, M., & Durán, L. (2015). Unpacking ideologies of linguistic purism: How dual language teachers make sense of everyday translanguaging. *International Multilingual Research Journal*, 9, 26–42.

Nash, K. T. (2013). Everyone sees color: Toward a transformative critical race framework of early literacy teacher education. *Journal of Transformative Education*, 11, 151–169.

Nash, K. T., & Sosinski, G. (2015). Leadership in a dual language community preschool: Small steps toward creating an assets-based program. In S. Long, M. Souto-Manning, & V. Vasquez (Eds.), *Courageous leadership: Administrators taking a stand for social justice in Early Childhood Education, practice and promise* (pp. 45–56). New York, NY: Teachers College Press.

Palmer, D. K., & Martínez, R. A. (2016). Developing biliteracy: What do teachers really need to know about language? *Language Arts*, 93, 379–385.

Palmer, D. K., Martínez, R. A., Mateus, S. G., & Henderson, K. (2014). Reframing the debate on language separation: Toward a vision for translanguaging pedagogies in the dual language classroom. *The Modern Language Journal*, 98, 757–772.

Paris, D. (2012). Culturally sustaining pedagogy: A needed change in stance, terminology, and practice. *Educational Researcher*, 41(3), 93–97.

Paris, D., & Alim, H. S. (2014). What are we seeking to sustain through culturally sustaining pedagogy? A loving critique forward. *Harvard Educational Review*, 84, 85–100.

Paris, D., & Alim, H. S. (2017). *Author interview by Larry Ferlazzo: Culturally sustaining pedagogies*. Retrieved from http://blogs.edweek.org/teachers/classroom_qa_with_larry_ferlazzo/2017/07/author_interview_culturally_sustaining_pedagogies.html?r=604476754.

Piña, P., Nash, K. T., Boardman, A., Polson, B., & Panther, L.(2015). Engaging teachers, families, and children in culturally relevant literacies. *Journal of Family Strengths*, 15(2), article 3. Retrieved from http://digitalcommons.library.tmc.edu/jfs/vol15/iss2/3/

Robinson, R., & Yaden, D. B. (1993). Chaos or nonlinear dynamics: Implications for reading research. *Literacy Research and Instruction*, 32(4), 15–23.

Rosa, J., & Flores, N. (2017). Do you hear what I hear? Raciolinguistic ideologies and culturally sustaining pedagogies. In D. Paris & H. S. Alim (Eds.), *Culturally sustaining pedagogies: Teaching and learning for justice in a changing world* (pp. 175–190). New York, NY: Teachers College Press.

Skiba, R. J., Simmons, A. B., Ritter, S., Gibb, A. C., Rausch, M. K., Cuadrado, J., & Chung, C. G. (2008). Achieving equity in special education: History, status, and current challenges. *Exceptional Children*, 74, 264–288.

Smith, P. H., & Murillo, L. A. (2015). Theorizing translanguaging and multilingual literacies through human capital theory. *International Multilingual Research Journal*, 9(1), 59–73.

Souto-Manning, M., & Martell, J. (2016). *Reading, writing, and talk: Inclusive teaching strategies for diverse learners, K–2*. New York, NY: Teachers College Press.

Sutcher, L., Darling-Hammond, L., & Carver-Thomas, D. (2016). *A coming crisis in teaching? Teacher supply, demand, and shortages in the US*. Learning Policy Institute. Retrieved from https://learningpolicyinstitute. org/product/coming-crisis-teaching

Torres, T. (n.d.). Personal communication.

United States Census. (2010). Retrieved from https://www.census.gov/programs-surveys/decennial-census/decade.html

Volk, D. (2013). "Contradictions, clashes, cominglings": The syncretic literacy projects of young bilinguals. *Anthropology & Education Quarterly*, 44, 234–252.

Volk, D. (2015). I'm going to see that they are something in life: Latino parents in two families as warm demanders. *Perspectives and Provocations in Early Childhood Education*, 3(5), 5–17.

Vygotsky, L. S. (1978). *Mind in society: The development of higher mental process*. Cambridge, MA: Harvard University Press.

Ware, F. (2006). Warm demander pedagogy: Culturally responsive teaching that supports a culture of achievement for African American students. *Urban Education*, 41, 427–456.

Wertheim, M. (2005). Crocheting the hyperbolic plane: An interview with David Henderson and Daina Taimina. *Cabinet*, no. 16. Retrieved from http://www.cabinetmagazine.org/issues/16/crocheting.php

Williams, C. (1994). *Arfarniad o ddulliau dysgu ac addysgu yng nghyd-destun addysg uwchradddwyieithog [An evaluation of teaching and learning methods in the context of bilingual secondary education]* (Unpublished PhD thesis). University of Wales, Bangor, UK.

Yaden, D. B. (2013). Personal communication.

Yaden, D. B., Tam, A., Madrigal, P., Brassell, D., Massa, J., Altamirano, L. S., & Armendariz, J. (2000). Early literacy for inner-city children: The effects of reading and writing interventions in English and Spanish during the preschool years. *The Reading Teacher*, 54, 186–189.

3

TOWARD CULTURALLY SUSTAINING PEDAGOGY

Engagements with Latina Mothers Through Latino/Latina Children's Literature

Julia López-Robertson with Mary Jade Haney

In Lak'ech is a Mayan principle that is an integral part of a poem written by Luis Váldez (1973) titled, 'Pensamiento Serpentino':

> "In Lak 'ech"
> Tú Eres mi otro yo.
> You are my other me.
> Si te hago daño a ti,
> If I do harm to you,
> Me hago daño a mí mismo.
> I do harm to myself.
> Si te amo y respeto,
> If I love and respect you,
> Me amo y respeto yo.
> I love and respect myself.

According to Váldez, the meaning of the phrase '*In Lak'ech*' is "affiliated with the Mayan definition of the human being, which they called 'huinik'lil' or 'vibrant being'" (http://vue.annenberginstitute.org/perspectives/lak'ech-you-are-my-other). The poem formed the foundation of our relationship as a dyad and all the work in which we engaged with teachers, children, and their families. Like Váldez (1971), we believe that we are all a part of the same universal vibration, a 'collective human being' that is responsible for each other and our actions.

In this chapter, we discuss our work as a dyad, the beliefs that guide our practice, and the projects in which we engaged; explorations with writing and photography, and explorations of Latino/Latina children's literature. We also provide background information about the process to provide a more complete picture of our work.

Meet the Authors

We are Mary Jade Haney and Julia López-Robertson. We met several years ago when Mary Jade was a student in Julia's doctoral seminar at the University of South Carolina. At the time, Mary Jade was the art teacher at Horrell Hill Elementary School.

Mary Jade connected deeply with Freire (2000) as explored in Julia's class and discussed the ways in which the banking concept of education was negatively impacting the children with whom she worked. She spoke passionately about her students and families and her desire to engage them in meaningful ways and invited Julia to a school-wide family literacy night to see it all for herself. Upon arrival at the school event, Julia was awed by the sheer number of families in attendance; there was nowhere to park, the middle school across the street served as overflow parking and that was completely packed—and she had arrived 30 minutes early! The attendance at the family literacy night is evidence, as N. González (2001) states, that "there is no need to interject into the community an interest in their children's education because *it is already there*" (p. 163; italics in original). Also of interest is the fact that attendance was multigenerational; numerous families brought grandparents and some even great-grandparents, thus connecting to the notion of a "collective genealogy of knowledge" (Holmes & González, 2017, p. 210) which respects elders' ways of knowing and making meaning. Julia felt very warmly welcomed by all members of the community and was even able to actively contribute as an interpreter for several of the Latino/Latina[1] families in attendance. The evening's events were centered on the "cultural, linguistic, and literate pluralism" (Alim & Paris, 2017, p. 13) of the school community and included reading aloud, singing, storytelling, and many stations for the families to visit and engage in with their children throughout the school. At the end of the evening, the families all gathered in the gymnasium where Ms. Satterwhite [the principal] thanked them for their participation in the evening's events and encouraged them to visit when they are able. She also reminded them that they did not need to wait until the next school-wide event to visit. Julia was immediately taken with the families and the rest, as they say, is history.

Mary Jade Haney

Mary Jade is an African American woman who was born and raised in South Carolina. She is a 21-year public-school educator, National Board-Certified Teacher, and the literacy coach at Horrell Hill Elementary School in Richland School District One. Mary Jade understands the art of teacher leadership and inspires children to creatively develop as inquisitive human beings through critical thinking, reading, writing, and communicating in authentic ways. She works collaboratively with educators, families, and students as their voices challenge inequities in educational spaces. An advocate for students, families, and community members, she believes all children have the potential to make positive and creative contributions to our world. In Figure 3.1, Mary Jade is working alongside Latina mothers on a response to literature. Mary Jade is an active participant in our literature discussions and is in the process of becoming bilingual, Spanish-English, because of her desire to communicate with and advocate for the Latino/Latina children and families at Horrell Hill.

Julia López-Robertson

Julia is a Spanish-speaking Latina teacher educator who spent 17 years as a bilingual first- and second-grade teacher in Boston, MA and in Tucson, AZ before moving to the University of South Carolina. She was born and raised in Boston, MA by a Colombian mother and Cuban father. Julia did not see herself, her language, or culture represented in a book until she was a graduate student at the University of Arizona. She is passionate about sharing Latino/Latina children's literature with Latino/Latina children and families (in particular) because she wants them to see themselves in the curriculum and in the pages of the books they read and talk about. In the photo, Julia is reading aloud *Niño Wrestles the World* (Morales, 2015) with the Latina mothers' group and their children (this engagement will be discussed in more detail later).

FIGURE 3.1 Mary Jade creating a response to literature.

FIGURE 3.2 Julia sharing Latino/Latina Literature with Latina mothers' group.

As a teacher researcher, Julia engaged her first- and second-grade students in discussions about critical social issues (cf. López-Robertson, 2011) and has continued that work in her role as a teacher educator. Julia's goals in working with children and their families are to present them with real representations of their experiences in books (López-Robertson with Haney, 2017); she believes that in doing so, the reader's sense of identity and self-empowerment is enhanced. She works with children, families, and current and preservice teachers to advance understandings about emerging bilingual/multilingual students and families and to support equitable teaching for all children, particularly English learners.

Beliefs Guiding Our Practice

Together we take a critical sociocultural approach (Freire & Macedo, 1987/2005; Vygotsky, 1980) to understanding the broader context of children's schooling (Reyes & Halcón, 2001) and believe that children's lived experiences must be made a part of school learning for them to be able to "transform their lived experiences into knowledge and use the already acquired knowledge as a process to unveil new knowledge" (Macedo, 2000, p. 19). We support the notion of a culturally sustaining pedagogy (Paris & Alim, 2014) where schools must situate the "linguistic, literate, and cultural practices of working-class communities—specifically poor communities of color—as resources and assets to honor, explore, and extend" (p. 87) and believe that in order to do this, schools must reconsider a 'one size fits all' stance to one that reflects "remixed and hybrid versions" (Paris & Alim, 2017, p. 4) of the linguistic, cultural, and community practices of their students and families.

We build on Freire and Macedo's (1987/2005) view of teaching and learning as a "relationship of learners to the world" (p. viii) and understand that learning is heavily influenced by social, cultural, and political forces (Nieto, 1999). While we know that knowledge of children's lives in their communities can have a profound impact on both curriculum and teaching practice as teachers build on what children bring to learning interactions (López-Robertson, 2012), we are very aware that "our challenge becomes to organize the teaching-learning process to the potential and not the perceived developmental level of our children" (Díaz & Flores, 2001, p. 31). We are not blind to the fact that there are educators who bring deficit views of minoritized children to their teaching; Paris & Alim (2014) remind us:

> Deficit approaches to teaching and learning have echoed across decades of education in the United States. Such approaches view the languages, literacies, and cultural ways of being of many students and communities of color as deficiencies to be overcome if they are to learn the dominant language, literacy, and cultural ways of being demanded in schools. (p. 87)

We offer that in order to counter these prevalent deficit-laden ways of teaching, educators need to "develop radical pedagogical structures that provide students with the opportunity to use their own reality as a basis of literacy" (Freire & Macedo, 1987/2005, p. 151). We argue that engaging students with carefully selected multicultural literature, "literature that is respectful and reflective of their life experiences" (López-Robertson with Haney, 2017, n.p.); "critically centering multilingual and multicultural heritage and community practices through actively building on student and community input" (Paris & Alim, 2017, p. 4); and intentionally engaging families in their children's schooling, they become "agents who can intervene and advocate on behalf of their children, and who can make adaptations and resist barriers to education" (Baquedano-López, Alexander, & Hernandez, 2013, p. 150) serve as examples of such radical pedagogical structures.

Context: Horrell Hill Elementary School

Located in Hopkins, South Carolina just 15 miles from the capital and the University of South Carolina in downtown Columbia, Horrell Hill Elementary is surrounded by working farms, several subdivisions, shopping centers, and older established neighborhoods. Horrell Hill serves 634 students in PreK–fifth grade; 72% of the school population are African American, 14% are White, 9% are two or more races, and 5% are Latino/Latina. Most of the school population is lower socio-economic status with 61% of the children receiving free and/or reduced lunch. Horrell Hill has had consistent and dedicated leadership; Ms. Parthenia Satterwhite has been the principal of Horrell Hill for over 25 years.

Ms. Satterwhite is very aware that "students are disenfranchised from learning because curricula fail to capitalize on their strengths and knowledge" (López-Robertson & Haney, 2016, p. 104); she trusts her teachers as professionals and encourages them to adapt district curriculum and create curriculum that incorporates the students' ways of knowing. Ms. Satterwhite believes that Horrell

Hill serves an important role in the community; more than merely a school, it is a "site for sustaining the cultural ways of being of communities of color" (Alim & Paris, 2017, p. 5); it is a gathering place where children and their families come together to celebrate milestones, participate in school events, and engage in learning and sharing knowledge.

Latino/Latina Family Engagement: The Foundation of Our Dyad Work

As we began our dyad work at Horrell Hill Elementary School, Immigration and Customs Enforcement was conducting raids in local farms, industry, and plants in the areas surrounding Horrell Hill. Many Latino/Latina families of children at the school were employed in the poultry plants, industries, and working farms and vulnerable to deportation. Upon learning that a raid had in fact occurred in one of the plants employing several families, Ms. Satterwhite became very concerned for their safety. Naturally, this raid had a critical impact on the school community, but it also led school leaders to consider what they actually knew about Latino/Latina families. Through talking with the families, Ms. Satterwhite learned about the "cultural misinterpretations and microaggressions" (López-Robertson & Haney, 2016, p. 105) they experienced and asked us to focus our work on creating a space where Latino/Latina families could join the school community, a space where they would feel welcomed and feel a sense of belonging; in essence she was asking us to "reimagine [Horrell Hill] as a site where diverse, heterogeneous practices are not only valued but sustained" (Alim & Paris, 2017, p. 3).

While, at that time, we operated from a culturally relevant conceptual base, we have since then been drawn to Paris and Alim's (2014) notion of culturally sustaining pedagogies "as the place where the 'beat drops'" (Ladson-Billings, 2014, p. 76) as we seek to go beyond relevance to a commitment "to perpetuate and foster—to sustain—linguistic, literate, and cultural pluralism as part of the democratic project of schooling" (Paris, 2012, p. 95). Alim and Paris (2017) named that commitment as they urged educators to "sustain the cultural ways of being of communities of color rather than eradicating them" (p. 2): Thus, we see our approach to Ms. Satterwhite's request as moving beyond the traditional view of '*how to*' involve parents in schools, to one that

> [r]epositioned the linguistic, literate, and cultural practices of working-class communities—specifically poor communities of color—as resources and assets to honor, explore, and extend in accessing White middle class dominant cultural norms of acting and being that are demanded in schools. (Alim & Paris, 2017, p. 4)

Our goal was to engage Latino/Latina families in the school community as active members rather than passive observers and do so in a manner that felt comfortable to them, thus supporting Alim and Paris's (2017) notion that "schooling [needs] to be a site for sustaining the cultural ways of being of communities of culture" (p. 5).

Literacies Alive! Fotos y Familias, Photos and Families

Like the family literacy night described at the beginning of the chapter, we invited all families to join us at an event we called: *Literacies Alive! Fotos y Familias, Photos and Families* (Figure 3.3). The goal of the event was to engage all families in "an evening of cultural enrichment/una noche enriquizente de cultura." The event was held on a Friday evening from 6:30 pm to 10:00 pm and included

Horrell Hill Elementary School

Invites You To

"An Evening of Cultural Enrichment""/Una noche enrequizente de cultura"

Come and learn Español and/or English

with family & friends through a variety of literacy engagements!

Vengan a aprender ingles o español con su familia y amigos

mientras están involucrados en actividades de literacia

Friday, viernes, May 18, 2012

6:30 p.m. - 10:00 p.m.

Horrell Hill Elementary School

(Cafeteria)

We are asking that a parent or parents plan to stay

and participate from 6:30 p.m.- 10:00 p.m. with their

child or children.

Pedimos que los padres de familia se queden todo el tiempo con su(s) niño/niños para

compartir en las varias actividades.

La cena se va servir a las 6:30p.m.

Dinner will be served at 6:30 p.m.

This is a FREE event!

If you and your family plan to attend, please contact:

¡El evento es GRATIS!

Si su familia desea asistir, favor de llamar a

Ms. Haney at (803) 783-5545 by Wednesday, May 16, 2012

Ms. Haney at (803) 783-5545

FIGURE 3.3 Literacies Alive! literacy night flyer.

dinner, conversation, stargazing, literacy stations, and cultural exchange. One of the engagements was a language exchange where we asked each person to find someone who spoke a language different than their own first language (Spanish/English). They were to have a small conversation and learn some basic information from their new friend; i.e. name, favorite color, favorite food.

Ms. Satterwhite led the engagement by talking with Julia in Spanish, while Mary Jade spoke with a Latina mother. A Spanish learner, Ms. Satterwhite demonstrated the same nervousness and excitement the families did! Through the event, Ms. Satterwhite was acting to "dismantle the artificial boundaries that exclude their language [Spanish] from public spaces … introducing bilingual practices into monolingual domains" (Bucholtz, Casillas, & Lee, 2017, p. 55), thus supporting culturally sustaining pedagogy's (CSP) aim to "reframe our thinking about language learning" (Rosa & Flores, 2017, p. 175). There was laughter and so much joy that evening; it was a huge success, a sentiment shared by many families.

Latina Mothers' Group

At the Literacies Alive! event, Julia and Mary Jade spoke with Latino/Latina families about the project and invited them to an informational meeting the following week at school; of the eight families invited, five joined us and the five were all mothers. We shared our goals with the mothers; to involve them actively in the school community and to enact a culturally sustaining pedagogy that positions their "linguistic practices as resources rather than deficits" (Rosa & Flores, 2017, p. 175) through a variety of engagements that would occur weekly in a small group setting at school. All seemed eager to participate. The mothers suggested that the best day for them to meet was Friday and they preferred the afternoon—this way they would not have to return to pick up their children at the end of the school day. It was decided that our meetings would take place three Fridays a month from 12:30 to 2:00 p.m. in the Literacy room.

One of the mothers expressed concerns about the children she was taking care of during the day; we let her know that she could bring the children and we would work with them too. We were particularly excited by the fact that we had mothers participating because we knew that they were "not often seen as resources within the household, schools do not often validate their experiences or draw on their multiple funds of knowledge" (N. González, 2001, p. 127). Over time, the Latina mothers' group provided them the space to learn about school, to interact with each other, and to engage in authentic discussions about their lives and life experiences and learn from each other. Mary Jade and Julia also learned a lot from the mothers; it was truly a reciprocal learning experience for all of us.

Explorations with Writing and Photography

One of our very first engagements was based on the book *The Best Part of Me* (Ewald, 2002). The book was created by Ewald in collaboration with teacher Lisa Lord and her third–fifth-grade students in a public elementary school in Durham, North Carolina. Ewald's black-and-white photographs of the children's favorite body parts are accompanied by the children's writing that explains why the body part depicted is their favorite. Using this book provided a great way for us to get to know each other and would also serve to strengthen our belief that we were building on what they already had; we were "sustaining the lifeways of communities who have been and continue to be damaged and erased through schooling" (Alim & Paris, 2017, p. 1).

As with all our meetings, Julia read the book aloud and since this book was only written in English and the mothers were English learners with varying knowledge of English, Julia translated the book as she read (López-Robertson, 2014). We talked about the book while Julia read, and she asked: "¿Cuál es la major parte de mí? What is my favorite part of me?" After some discussion, we gave the mothers a camera and asked them to photograph each other's favorite part. The room was filled with laughter and excitement as we engaged in this activity. After the photographs had been taken, we printed them and gave them

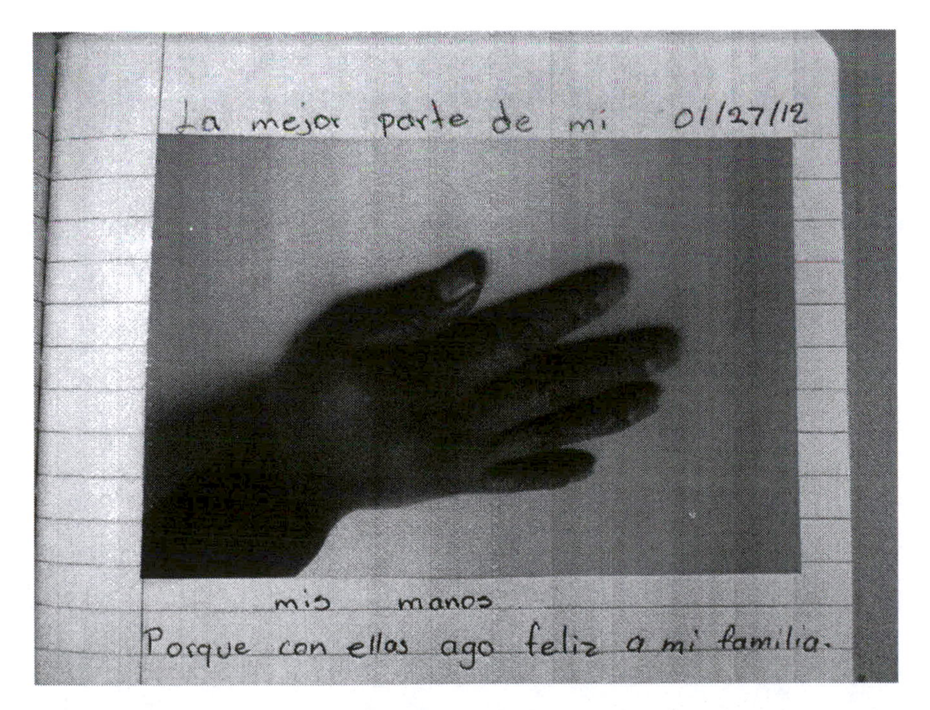

FIGURE 3.4 Journal entry: "The Best Part of Me."

to their respective owner. We then glued each photograph in a notebook and asked the mothers to briefly write about their favorite body part. Figure 4 is an example of one of the pages. Jessica wrote, "My hands are my favorite part because with them I make my family happy." We continued this work with the children when they joined us and made a book titled *La major parte de mi*/The Best Part of Me.

Working with photographs continued in another engagement where the mothers and their children created a school ABC book. We began by writing the alphabet on the whiteboard and together with the children, discussing which objects in school could be represented in the book. Once we completed the alphabet chart, each mother and child chose their letters, took their camera, and off they went to photograph the school. Over the next few weeks, we continued to work on the bilingual book—a project that supports Paris and Alim's (2014) notion that CSP in educational practice is centered on learners "maintaining their multiple ways of speaking and being" (p. 89) so as to value their "linguistically and culturally dexterous ways of being" (p. 91).

Written Responses to Latino/Latina Children's Literature

The next book we shared was *Hairs/Pelitos* by Sandra Cisneros (1997). This bilingual picture book engages the reader with vibrant illustrations that depict the different types of hair of each family member.

We laughed about the illustrations and talked about family members in the United States and in Mexico and the mothers shared how yes, indeed, all family members can have different types of hair and yet, still belong to the same family. After talking about the book, Mary Jade and Julia asked the mothers to write a brief response to the book. Figure 3.5 is one of the responses; she writes,

> The little girl tells her mom about soft hair and 'scary' hair (one of the illustrations was papá's hair that stood up like a broom). The little girl felt the love that she had for her mom and family. And all the boys and girls and the parents had different hair, some curly, straight, and scary.

In the beginning, the mothers were a little shy about writing; Yazmin said, "Pues, no sé escribir muy bien/I don't know how to write that well"—with our encouragement, however, the mothers wrote. Julia and Mary Jade explained that they were not looking for proper sentence structure or grammar; rather the interest was in the meaning that their writing conveyed. By creating these opportunities to think and write about personal connections to books, we were enacting a CSP as our focus was on the mother's "repertoires of practice— the ways of engaging in activities stemming from participation in a range of cultural practices, as well as the learning that occurs in the development of those repertoires" (Gutiérrez & Johnson, 2017, p. 251).

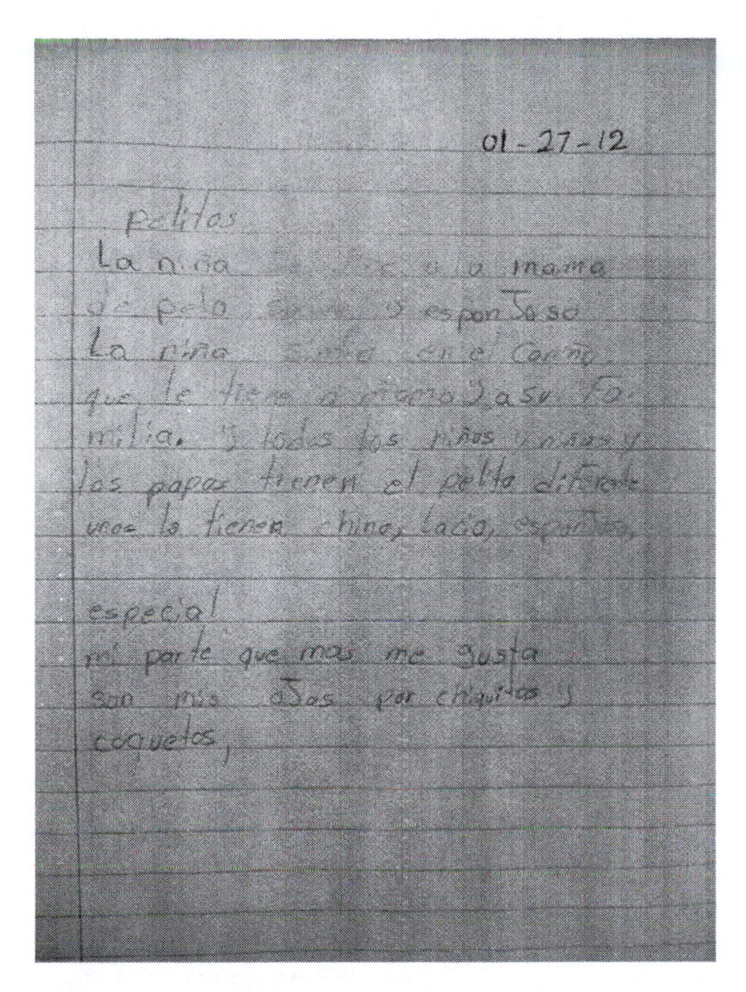

FIGURE 3.5 Response to *Pelitos*.

Explorations of Latino/Latina Children's Literature

We understand that the use of authentic literature does not occur in every classroom and recognize that this lack of representation is entrenched in the reality that very frequently "existing classroom practices underestimate and constrain what Latino/Latina and other children are able to display intellectually" (González, Moll, & Amanti, 2005, p. 27); for this reason, our work with the Latino/Latina families in the mothers' group was grounded upon the use of Latino/Latina children's literature. A prominent feature of CSP is that instruction connects present learning to the histories of racial, ethnic, and linguistic communities, and to the histories of neighborhoods and cities (Paris & Alim, 2017); exposure to and engagement with Latino/Latina literature allowed our families and children to access such instruction. Figure 3.6 contains a sample list of books we used.

Title	*Author*
What Can You Do with a Paleta?	Carmen Tafolla
In My Family/En Mi Familia	Carmen Lomas Garza
Dear Primo: A Letter to My Cousin	Duncan Tonatiuh
Just a Minute	Yuyi Morales
Just in Case	Yuyi Morales
My Abuelita	Yuyi Morales
Nochecita	Yuyi Morales
My Colors, My World	Maya Gonzalez
My Diary from Here to There	Maya Gonzalez

FIGURE 3.6 Titles of some of the children's books we used.

One of the books that brought a lot of joy and discussion was *Niño Wrestles the World* (Morales, 2015). In the story, the main character, Niño, is a successful *luchador* (wrestler) until the very end of the book where he is defeated by his baby sisters! One discussion around the book was about childhood memories that involved wrestling:

JAZMÍN: Esto me recuerda como mis hermanos se lo pasaba luchando en la casa. Hay, como hacían reguero. Tiraban cojines, ropa, zapatos, todo lo que encontraban.

[This reminds me of when my brothers would spend the day wrestling at home. Oh, what a mess they would make. They would throw cushions, clothes, shoes, everything they found.]

BETSY: Hay, sí, mi hermano mayor, que bruto era a veces. Me lanzaba allá en esa cama-no sé cómo nunca me rompí un hueso.

[Oh, yes, my older brother, he was a little rough sometimes. He would throw me on that bed, I don't know how I never broke a bone.]

IMELDA: Que sí que, una vez Rafael me dio un tirón en el sofá que casi me quebré la muñeca.

[Really, once Rafael threw me on the sofa so hard that I almost broke my wrist.]

REYNA: Sí, y me recuerdo los fines de semana, con la tele y a mirar la lucha libre. ¡A mi papá le encantaba-hasta una vez me llevo a una lucha!

[Yes, and I remember the weekends with the TV on and watching wrestling. My dad loved it, he even took me once!]

JESSICA: ¡Si, y ahora que, yo aquí detrás de estos chamacos que no me anden luchando en la casa!

[Yes, and now what, I am after these kids telling them not to wrestle in the house.]

BETSY: [Riéndose] ¡Mira cómo es la vida!

[[Laughing] Look how life is!]

In the excerpt above, the mothers were reminiscing about their childhood and the very popular *Lucha Libre*. When I read this book to English speakers, they often equate it with World Wrestling Entertainment (WWE); however, "a story told in one language conveys a very different picture when it is translated" (N. González, 2001, p. 128). The same can be said about cultural events such as *Lucha Libre*! Later in the same discussion, the mothers commented on how for them, this was nothing like WWE:

BETSY: Al niño le gusta mira lo americano, eso de WWE. A mi no me gusta para nada.

[He [her son] likes to watch the American [wrestling], the WWE. I don't like it at all.]

JAZMÍN: Eso de los americanos tiene mucho sexo, las mujeres andan por allí...

[The American [wrestling] has too much sex, the women are there...]

JESSICA: Si casi sin ropa. No, para mí no es igual. Nuestra lucha es más como teatro tiene más de nuestra cultura.

[Yes, with hardly any clothes. No, for me it's not the same. Our wrestling is more theatre like and has more about our culture.]

There was another type of discussion that surrounded this book as well. We mentioned above that the mothers brought concerns about their children's schooling to us once they felt comfortable doing so. Jessica shared with us that at a parent–teacher conference the week prior, her son Luis, a first-grader, was being considered for retention because he could not read. His teacher shared that he was disruptive, could not recite the alphabet, and showed no interest in reading at all. Jessica explained that she took him and his brother (a fourth-grader) to the library every week where she watched him pick out several books and read them to her [in English] at home. Also at the library, there were volunteers for the children to read with and Luis did so and did it well. Jessica was surprised at hearing what the teacher said because she was seeing quite the opposite from her son.

She brought this up during our discussion because, as can be seen in the photograph, (Figure 3.7), Luis is very interested in the book. Understanding and empathizing with Jessica's concerns about Luis's reading, we had the other families engage in an artistic response while we sat with Luis and Jessica. Julia handed Luis the book and asked him to read when he was ready. He looked at his mother, at Julia, at Mary Jade, and then started reading. He read the entire book with fluency and intonation and even added additional sound effects. She had tears in her eyes when she said, "Yo sabía que el niño podia leer/I knew my son could read." Mary Jade asked Luis to do a retelling of the story—he gave a detailed retelling and offered predictions on what could happen in book 2 (*Rudas: Niño's Horrendous Hermanitas*, Morales, 2016), he remembered that we were reading it next week.

FIGURE 3.7 Reading *Niño Wrestles the World.*

As the literacy coach, Mary Jade offered to speak with the teacher on her behalf. Jessica declined and explained,

> Con el poquito de inglés que puedo hablar, voy a hablar con la maestra. Si es que no me entiende, Ms. Haney, tú le puedes hablar. With the little bit of English that I can speak, I am going to speak with the teacher. And if she doesn't understand me, Ms. Haney you can speak with her.

Betsy validated Jessica, saying, "¡Hay muchacha, yo se que te van entender!/Girl, I know she [the teacher] will understand you."

We were very careful to have our families' *confianza* (González et al., 1993), a mutual trust "which is re-established or confirmed with each exchange and leads to the development of long-term relationships" (p. 3) before we engaged in any type of discussions. We feel that this *confianza* allowed Jessica to share her concerns about the incorrect assessment of her child's reading ability with us. More importantly, she felt the confidence to advocate for her child and "resist barriers to [his] education" (Baquedano-López et al., 2013, p. 150).

Out of School Experiences

Ms. Satterwhite was keenly aware of and challenged commonly held myths about Latino/Latina families (i.e., they don't care, are uninterested, and they do not contribute positively to their children's education) and was deliberate in the manner in which she strengthened the active participation of Latino/Latina families at Horrell Hill. One way she did this was to approve our request to take the Latina mothers and their children on field trips.

Field trips provide students the opportunity to extend their classroom learning by visiting locations and engaging in experiences that cannot be reproduced in the classroom. The experiential learning taking place on field trips allows students to make links with prior life experiences (Behrendt & Franklin, 2014, p. 236) while connecting to the community. For immigrant families facing the task of building lives for themselves and their families in an unknown culture (Quiocho & Daoud, 2006), the field trips provide a route to learning about the new community and culture. We visited the State Museum, the University of South Carolina, the Main Branch of our public library and a local park, and the Zoo and Botanical Gardens. While on these field trips, we engaged in discussions about history, made connections to books we had read at school, and enjoyed being together and learning more about each other.

Prior to leaving school, the mothers and their children were given cameras and asked to take photographs during our excursions that would later be used to create something artistic.

Unbeknownst to the families our zoo has Botanical Gardens. Our trip to the Gardens provided an extra adventure; visiting the gardens required a long walk (on a very hot day) or a ride on the tram. We rode the tram! While on the tram crossing the bridge leading to the gardens the mothers made connections to the rivers in their home towns and to a book we had recently read, *I Know the River Loves Me/Yo sé que el rio me ama* (M. C. González, 2012). One mother commented, "Que lindo, me recuerda del rio de mi pueblo en donde nos pasábamos muy lindo toda la familia/How pretty, this reminds me of the river in my town where the whole family had lovely times." Another added, "Sí, también del librito con la niña y el rio/Yes, and also the book with the little girl and the river." The children were so excited during the tram ride and took an incredible number of pictures of the tram; the river; their mothers telling stories, and of course, there were selfies with the river and/or tram in the background.

A few weeks after our visit to the Gardens the mothers and children were working on the slide show of the visit. Each of their notebooks contained the text they wrote to accompany a slide. Jazmín and Tania (her second-grade daughter) had four photographs they were writing about. Tania explained to her mother that she would write in English and her mother would write in Spanish. As they were writing, Jazmín commented how surprised she was at Tania's ability to write in English because her writing score on the report card that had been distributed a few days prior was so low. Tania commented, "Mami, lo que escribimos es tan boring [*sic*]. Ella nos pone unas palabras y hay que copiarlas o nos hace leer libros también que son boring [*sic*]/Mami, what we write is so boring. She makes us copy some words or she makes us read boring books." Jessica jumped in and reminded them about what happened with her son and suggested that Jazmín go speak with the teacher. A few weeks later, Jazmín shared that she had gone to speak with the teacher and had taken their notebook to show her Tania's work. The teacher, Jazmín said, was surprised to see the amount and quality of Tania's writing. Jazmín suggested that the teacher might include more personally interesting topics for Tania to write about. At the end of that term, about nine weeks after our visit to the Gardens, Jazmín walked into our group meeting with Tania's report card and pointed to her writing score, which was considerably higher than the last one.

Culturally sustaining pedagogy calls for students, families, teachers, and communities to engage with content and instruction that connects present learning to the histories of racial, ethnic, and linguistic communities, and to the histories of neighborhoods and cities of which they are a part (Paris & Alim, 2017). Taking these field trips provided the families the opportunity to connect with and highlight the wealth of the community while also engaging in the learning process with their children.

Culminating Celebration with the Families

The Latina mothers organized a celebration for our last meeting of the school year. They asked each of us to prepare a dish to share with the group that represented something about our culture. We had a table of delicious foods; tamales, salads, desserts, salsa, and a homemade cake to celebrate 'Feliz día de amigos/happy friends' day' (Figure 3.8). Somehow the mothers learned that it was Ms. Satterwhite's birthday. They asked us to call her to our meeting room. Ms. Satterwhite walked

FIGURE 3.8 Feliz día amigos/Happy friends' day homemade cake.

into the dark Literacy Room and was a little startled when she heard "SURPRISE!" What followed was a joyous luncheon and dancing that celebrated our year, a principal who prioritized them, and our new friendships.

Insights from Our Work Together

The work in which we engaged with the mothers would not have been possible *or sustainable* if we did not have the support of a principal who is truly invested in the learning and well-being of all her children and their families. Ms. Satterwhite worries about the "labels that send indelibly destructive messages about self-worth and capability" (López-Robertson, & Haney, 2016, p. 104) and, in response, initiates, supports, and engages in experiences that challenge negative and inaccurate representations. Furthermore, our work was about a mutual relationship with the mothers and was built upon trust, respect for our relationship, patience and time, and love. Ms. Satterwhite's support for the work as a school administrator cannot be underestimated as we consider *what* it takes to sustain this kind of teaching and the normalization of children's languages and cultures in the school.

Trust

Foundational to all our work is trust. Trust, writes Freire (2000), "is contingent on the evidence which one party provides the others of his true, concrete intentions; it cannot exist if that party's words do not coincide with their actions" (p. 91). The poem at the opening of our chapter, "In Lak'ech" (Valdez, 1973), speaks to the notion of trust and responsibility; "tú eres mi otro yo,/you are my other me." As a dyad we share that sense of trust and responsibility with each other and it also carries over into our work with our Latino/Latina families. Because we work with a vulnerable community—a community that lives in fear of deportation due to the political climate in which we live—we take the trust they have in us very seriously. Families know that we are working in their best interest and trust that we advocate for them and their children. Without trust, there exists no possibility for the transformational work or the "radical pedagogical structures" to emerge.

Relationships

Together with trust, is the understanding that none of our work would be possible without first having established a relationship with families. Holmes and González (2017) explain that Indigenous pedagogies and methodologies have been discredited by Western academia and ask that we "think more deeply and begin to dwell more profoundly with some of these critically relevant pedagogies of survival" (p. 212); value and discipline of the collective, the value and discipline of visiting, value and discipline of relationship, and the value of slowness and deliberateness. We found many parallels in the work with Latino/Latina families and connected greatly with the value and discipline of relationship. Holmes and González (2017) explain that "the ultimate value and discipline of relationship embodies the utmost respect, care, and consideration for the ways one carries oneself into relations with others" (p. 215). For us this meant giving time for the relationship with our families to grow, having patience that things were not going to happen immediately and understanding that we were not in control; we were following the lead of our families.

Patience and Time

At times we became frustrated because it did seem that things were taking forever! We learned to have patience and give time for things to unfold naturally. We did not simply begin talking about critical social issues such as immigration, linguicism, and racism with our families instantly; our mothers did not bring concerns with their children's schooling nor they did share personal stories of struggles, and later accomplishments, right away. It took time and patience to cultivate relationships and build trust; we continued to organize engagements and invite our families and we continued to demonstrate respect—for their lives, for their ways of knowing, and for the knowledge they were imparting on their children. And slowly, we became 'una familia'/ a family, as a few of our mothers commented.

Dyad Relationship

Our dyad relationship was built upon the same principles as the ones in which we approached our families; trust, respect for our relationship, patience and time, and love. We felt a mutual respect and an understanding that we would grow as a team through engaging the children and families in CSP. We trusted that we were in this together, that we could question each other honestly, and that we would see the project through to the end. We gave each other the gift of patience and time; there were times when our schedules would not allow for any flexibility and when phone calls and emails went unanswered. During these times, we never questioned our commitment to each other and the project; we knew that we would persevere. We were patient with each other and never questioned our commitment to our families, our project, and each other. Regardless of the hectic school and personal schedules, we knew that our families were our priority and that we would make it all work. Perhaps because neither of us had experienced education that valued our own linguistic, racial, or cultural heritage and know the importance of this for children of color, we are both deeply committed to culturally relevant pedagogies that are sustained. These commitments also allowed us to become closer as we spent more time together and as engaged the mothers in our project; learning to be patient with each other and value each other's expertise, background, and knowledge as well as that of the children and their families.

Closing Thoughts

We liken our work to that of weaving; each of the strings come together to make something beautiful while maintaining their originality. During a discussion of *Él tapiz de abuela/ Abuela's Weave* (Castañeda, 1995) Reyna, a mother, commented that our group was like a tapestry: "es como cuando uno está tejiendo un tapiz, cada quien tiene su hilo, y se une en una belleza de tapiz/it is like when you are weaving a tapestry, everyone has their string and it is joined in a beautiful tapestry." She is right, like a tapestry we each contribute something, something unique to each of us, and create one beautiful item.

We respect, admire, and love the Latina mothers. Our goal as a dyad was to create a space where the Latina mothers and the children's families could join the school community as active participants; a safe space where they would feel welcomed and a sense of belonging. By foregrounding engagements with Latino/Latina children's literature, the Latina mothers were able to see themselves in books and were able to "find within a book the truth of their own experiences instead of stereotypes and misrepresentations" (Fox & Short, 2003, p. 21). We had conversations about issues in the books, and the Latina mothers shared these books and conversations with their children in Spanish. Sharing these books with the Latina mothers also let them know that there are books that reflect their lives, language, and culture and that it is important to "sustain the lifeways of communities who have been and continue to be damaged and erased through schooling" (Alim & Paris, 2017, p. 1).

At the end of the day, our work at Horrell Hill is about love: "Love constitutes an intentional spiritual act of consciousness that emerges and matures through our social and material practices, as we work to live, learn, and labor together...as we seek new possibilities for transformation" (Darder, 2015, p. 49). Essential to that love is working to sustain pedagogies can "reframe our thinking about language learning" among Latino/Latina students and position students' "linguistic practices as resources rather than deficits" (Rosa & Flores, 2017, p. 175). We close our chapter asking what will take to make this kind of teaching foundational to teacher education programs and PreK–Grade 12, undergraduate and graduate schooling. How do we ensure that it does not continue to be reflected in the teaching of a teacher here and a teacher educator there but as a necessary and complete transformation in schools? This means building the convictions and the know-how to remain steadfast in our commitment to changing the ingrained structures of so many schools that are grounded in Eurocratic worldviews and thereby silence and oppress large populations of students while miseducating all students. When schools are grounded in the richness of all the students' heritage, culture, and families, they transform from environments that only work for some students, to an extension of the community that pulls all students forward.

Note

1 Julia López-Robertson does not use the term *Latinx* as used in other parts of this volume because she self-identifies as Latina and prefers to use the gendered forms of the word (e.g., Latino/Latina) when discussing families, literature, etc. It is not uncommon in communities of Color for people to use various terms to refer to themselves. These varying identifications are indicative of the complexity, sophistication, and advancement of languages, cultures, nationalities, and overall identities.

References

Alim, H. S., & Paris, D. (2017). What is culturally sustaining pedagogy and why does it matter? In D. Paris & H. S. Alim (Eds.), *Culturally sustaining pedagogies: Teaching and learning for justice in a changing world* (pp. 1–24). New York, NY: Teachers College Press.

Baquedano-López, P., Alexander, R. A., & Hernandez, S. J. (2013). Equity issues in parental and community involvement in schools: What teacher educators need to know. *Review of Research in Education*, 37, 149–182.

Behrendt, M., & Franklin, T. (2014). A review of research on school field trips and their value in education. *International Journal of Environmental & Science Education*, 9, 235–245.

Bucholz, M., Casillas, D. I., & Lee, J. S. (2017). Language and culture as sustenance. In D. Paris & H. S. Alim (Eds.), *Culturally sustaining pedagogies: Teaching and learning for justice in a changing world* (pp. 43–60). New York, NY: Teachers College Press.

Castañeda, O. (1995). *Abuelas weave*. New York, NY: Lee and Low Books.

Cisneros, S. (1997). *Hairs/Pelitos*. New York, NY: Dragonfly Books.

Darder, A. (2015). *Freire and education*. New York, NY: Routledge.

Díaz, E., & Flores, B. (2001). Teacher as sociocultural, sociohistorical mediator: Teaching to the potential. In M. Reyes & J. J. Halcón (Eds.), *The best for our children: Critical perspectives on literacy for Latino students* (pp. 29–47). New York, NY: Teachers College Press.

Ewald, W. (2002). *The best part of me: Children talk about their bodies in pictures and words*. New York, NY: Little, Brown Books for Young Readers.

Fox, D. L., & Short, K. G. (2003). *Stories matter: The complexity of cultural authenticity in children's literature*. Urbana, IL: National Council of Teachers of English.

Freire, P. (2000). *Pedagogy of the oppressed* (30th anniv.). New York, NY: Continuum.

Freire, P., & Macedo, D. (1987/2005). *Literacy: Reading the word and the world*. New York, NY: Routledge.

González, M. C. (2012). *I know the river loves me/yo sé que el rio me ama*. New York, NY: Lee and Low Publishers.

González, N. (2001). *I am my language: Discourses of women and children in the borderlands*. Tucson, AZ: University of Arizona Press.

González, N., Moll, L., & Amanti, C. (Eds.). (2005). *Fund of knowledge: Theorizing practices in households and classrooms*. Mahwah, NJ: Erlbaum.

González, N., Moll, L., Floyd-Tenery, M., Rivera, A., Rendon, P., Gonzales, R., & Amanti, C. (1993). *Teacher research on funds of knowledge: Learning from households* (Report 6). Retrieved from National Center for Research on Cultural Diversity and Second Language Learning website: https://ncela.ed.gov/files/rcd/BE019122/EPR6_Teacher_Research_on_Funds.pdf

Gutiérrez, K. D., & Johnson, P. (2017). Understanding identity sampling and cultural repertoires: Advancing learning in justice pedagogies. In D. Paris & H. S. Alim (Eds.), *Culturally sustaining pedagogies: Teaching and learning for justice in a changing world* (pp. 247–260). New York, NY: Teachers College Press.

Holmes, A., & González, N. (2017). Finding sustenance: An indigenous relational pedagogy. In D. Paris & H. S. Alim (Eds.), *Culturally sustaining pedagogies: Teaching and learning for justice in a changing world* (pp. 207–224). New York, NY: Teachers College Press.

Ladson-Billings, G. (2014). Culturally relevant pedagogy 2.0: a.k.a. the remix. *Harvard Educational Review*, 84, 74–84.

López-Robertson, J. (2011). "Yo el otro día vi, um, un mojadito": Young Latino children connecting with Friends from the Other Side. *New England Reading Association Journal*, 46(2), 52–59.

López-Robertson, J. (2012). "Esta página me recordó": Young Latinas using personal life stories as tools for meaning-making. *Bilingual Research Journal*, 35, 217–233.

López-Robertson, J. (2014). My gift to you is my language: Spanish is the language of my heart. In B. Kabuto & P. Martens (Eds.), *Linking families, learning, and schooling: Parent-researcher perspectives* (pp. 80–91). New York, NY: Routledge.

López-Robertson, J., & Haney, M. J. (2016). Making it happen: Risk-taking and relevance in a rural elementary school. In S. Long, M. Souto-Manning, & V. M. Vasquez (Eds.), *Courageous leadership in early childhood education: Taking a stand for social justice* (pp. 102–112). New York, NY: Teachers College Press.

López-Robertson, J., with Haney, M. J. (2017). Their eyes sparkled: Building classroom community through multicultural literature. *Journal of Children's Literature*, 43, 48–54. Macedo, D. (2000). Introduction. In P. Freire, *Pedagogy of the oppressed* (pp. 11–27). New York, NY: Continuum Press.

Morales, Y. (2015). *Niño wrestles the world*. New York, NY: Square Fish Publishers.

Morales, Y. (2016). *Rudas: Niño's horrendous hermanitas*. New York, NY: Roaring Brook Press.

Nieto, S. (1999). *The light in their eyes: Creating multicultural learning communities*. New York, NY: Teachers College Press.

Paris, D. (2012). Culturally sustaining pedagogy: A needed change in stance, terminology, and practice. *Educational Researcher*, 41(3), 93–97.

Paris, D., & Alim, H. S. (2014). What are we seeking to sustain through culturally sustaining pedagogy? A loving critique forward. *Harvard Educational Review*, 84, 85–100.

Paris, D., & Alim, H. S. (2017). *Culturally sustaining pedagogies: Teaching and learning for justice in a changing world*. New York, NY: Teachers College Press.

Quiocho, A. M., & Daoud, A. M. (2006). Dispelling myths about Latino parent participation in schools. *The Educational Forum*, 70, 255–267.

Reyes, M., & Halcón, J. J. (2001). *The best for our children: Critical perspectives on literacy for Latino students*. New York, NY: Teachers College Press.

Rosa, J., & Flores, N. (2017). Do you hear what I hear? Raciolinguistic ideologies and culturally sustaining pedagogies. In D. Paris & H. S. Alim (Eds.), *Culturally sustaining pedagogies: Teaching and learning for justice in a changing world* (pp. 175–190). New York, NY: Teachers College Press.

Váldez, L. (1973). *Pensamiento Serpentino: A Chicano approach to the theater of reality*. N.P.: Cucaracha Publications.

Vygotsky, L. S. (1980). *Mind in society: The development of higher psychological processes*. Cambridge, MA: Harvard University Press.

4

TOGETHER ENSURING STUDENTS' VOICES ARE HEARD, STORIES ARE TOLD, AND LEGACIES ARE PUT INTO ACTION

Bilal Polson and Alicia Arce-Boardman

Walk into our World

Maya Angelou (1997) once wrote, "There is no greater agony than bearing an untold story inside you." As you walk onto the campus of Northern Parkway School in Uniondale, New York you will see a large, beautiful, landmark school building reminiscent of the school dwellings constructed in the New York City schools by Charles B. J. Snyder in the early 20th century. The vibration and energy of Northern Parkway School is indicative of the community and families of the children who attend the school. The high ceilings, insightful bulletin boards, and vibrant colors painted on the walls give clear indication that this is not only a place for learning and celebration. Our intent is to announce to all children that this is a place where untold stories can be unearthed, a safe haven, recognizing that announcements are empty without the dispositions and pedagogies to back them up. Practices described in this chapter reflect work toward that end. In the classrooms, there are variations of living and learning spaces that include tables, desks, and specialized seating that have been customized and organized according to the needs of each classroom community. In each of the learning spaces are classroom libraries dominated by multicultural book collections that reflect people across racial, ethnic, and linguistic groups with a particular focus on titles, characters, authors, and illustrators that reflect the students in the classroom.

Our school, Northern Parkway, serves 810 students, 30% of whom are emergent bilingual and whose families' home languages are Spanish and Haitian Creole and who are typically from the Caribbean and South and Central America. The school is located about 20 miles outside of the New York Metropolitan area on Long Island. Like other suburbs in the Northeastern seaboard, Uniondale, New York continues to experience growth in its population of students who are adding to their linguistic repertoires. The school district has approximately 7200 students. Northern Parkway School is one of five elementary schools in the district. There are 810 students in grades K through 5. The student population is approximately 60% Latinx, 38% African American, 1% European American, and 1% Asian. Almost 80% of the students receive free or reduced lunch. The leadership team at Northern Parkway School is comprised of one principal (Bilal) and two assistant principals, who, representing the community racially and ethnically, are African American and Latinx. Northern Parkway School was recognized as New York State School of Character in 2015 and a National School of Character in 2016. Spanish is the home language of all students in Alicia's classroom. Alicia uses Spanish and English to deliver the instructional content in her room. Arce-Boardman and Polson use the term children of Color to identify Black, Latinx, Asian, and Indigenous Natives, and African, African American, and Black will be used to identify children of African heritage (Gates, 2011; Van Ausdale & Feagin, 2001).

Working as a dyad partnership, we fostered reciprocal learning and shared leadership through our collaborative work in driving culturally relevant, culturally responsive, and culturally sustaining literacy instruction and curriculum design, determining how to ensure students' interests, voices, and stories were heard and expressed in everyday structures like morning meeting (Brice-Heath & Mangiola, 1991; Campano, 2007), and reading and writing workshop. This chapter focuses on how we, Alicia Arce-Boardman, a second-grade teacher in a bilingual education classroom, and Bilal Polson, the schools' K–5 principal and assistant principal at the start of the project, used practitioner inquiry research methodologies (Campano, 2007; Mills, 2011) to learn together about how culturally relevant (Ladson-Billings, 1995), culturally responsive (Gay, 2010), and culturally sustaining (Paris & Alim, 2017) teaching influenced students' literacy growth in Alicia's second-grade classroom. We draw from Gloria Ladson-Billings' (1995) explanation of culturally relevant pedagogy as anchored in developing students' academic achievement, cultural competence, and critical consciousness. We embrace Geneva Gay's (2010) description of culturally responsive teaching as that which uses "the cultural knowledge, prior experiences, frames of reference and performances styles of ethnically diverse students to make learning encounters more relevant and effective for them" (p. 31). And we have also come to understand Django Paris and Samy Alim's (2017) articulation of culturally sustaining pedagogy as teaching that, "seeks to perpetuate and foster—to sustain—linguistic, literary and cultural pluralism as part of schooling for positive transformation" (Paris & Alim, 2017, p. 1). To illuminate our work, we share five classroom examples of culturally relevant, responsive, and sustaining curricula generated as a result of listening and attending to students' voices, languages, and backgrounds as the heart and soul of literacy curriculum (Bomer, 2010; Darder, 1991). Those stories are prefaced by discussions of our own backgrounds and the evolution of our relationship as a dyad.

Meet the Authors: Alicia and Bilal

Alicia Arce-Boardman was born and raised in Queens, New York. She grew up in a very close-knit Latinx family. Her family home was shared with many of her aunts as they emigrated from Paraguay, South America throughout Alicia's childhood. She moved to Long Island as a teenager after graduating high school. She received her undergraduate degree from the State University of New York at Stony Brook in Psychology. Before receiving her graduate degree in Childhood Education and becoming an educator, she worked in the field of social services. As a single mother, Alicia knew it was important to be able to support her daughter; therefore a stable job was vital. After being in the field of social work for a year, she returned to school to receive her graduate degree in Childhood Education from Dowling College. Alicia began teaching in the Uniondale School district in 2008 and received a Bilingual Education extension to her teaching certificate in 2010. Alicia was always drawn to the ideas and practices of culturally relevant teaching even before she could name it as such. It was important to her that the children in her classroom always felt that they were important and had a voice in the classroom. Alicia did not have that kind of experience when she in school. As a fluent Spanish speaker who was becoming bilingual, Alicia was often told that she was not allowed to speak Spanish in school, only English. This made her feel bashful and diminished her confidence. As a result, she did not want the same kind of degradation for her children and her students, and so she works to make sure that they are not silenced in school.

Bilal Polson was born and raised in Bay Shore, New York, a small suburban town on Long Island. Bilal identifies as African American and African Latino, a Black man whose roots are connected to Africa and Panama. Bilal's mother is African American and his dad, who emigrated from Panama, identifies as Black. When he was 13, Bilal moved to live with his maternal grandparents and aunt in Brooklyn to attend LaGuardia High School of the Performing Arts in New York City. Bilal received his undergraduate degree from New York University. He then studied Movement Therapy at the University of California, Los Angeles and holds degrees in Education from Adelphi University and Educational Administration from Hofstra University. Bilal received his doctoral degree in Educational Leadership at Hofstra University in May 2013. Like Alicia, Bilal was drawn to the tenets of culturally relevant as well as culturally sustaining pedagogies long before he knew them to be named as such. Practices that are grounded in a belief in the relevance of every student's family, community, heritage, and language *and* that work to sustain diverse ways of being in schools, students' lives, and the greater society are important to him as a school leader, researcher, and parent. This stems from the fact that Bilal's early childhood school experiences were not amenable to his learning needs. His school was not set up to meet the needs of an energetic, kinesthetic learner who needed additional support with reading. The combining influences of his physical education teacher, elementary school principal, and

FIGURE 4.1 Alicia Arce-Boardman.

dance teacher, who established a system and program to sustain his learning styles and habits, helped build Bilal's strong educational foundation. His academic outcomes improved when teaching became culturally relevant and thereby motivated and sustained Bilal's learning in school. As an early childhood school principal (vice-principal at the time of the study), Bilal observes daily how students benefit from teaching and learning that is culturally relevant. He works with his staff to make changes in school policies and curriculum, instruction, and assessment practices to make sure that those changes are not just relevant and responsive to students, but are sustained.

The Dyad Partnership

As a PDCRT dyad, establishing our roles as co-mentors to learn from each other and lead together was a particularly important issue to address. Since Bilal served as an administrator in the school where Alicia served as a teacher, it was easy to fall into a top-down model. At the time, Alicia was also a participant in Bilal's dissertation research, so there was a power dynamic that needed to be negotiated,

FIGURE 4.2 Bilal Polson.

along with establishing a working relationship after finding ourselves as players in the traditional university/school leader–teacher hierarchy, which was also defined by cultural histories and expectations. For example, Alicia felt it was respectful to call Bilal "Dr. Polson" and felt that his role and expertise meant that he would take the lead in idea generation and concept development. Eventually Alicia began initiating many of the ideas that she and Bilal would work on together; Alicia's instructional approach would serve to guide to illustrate what authentic culturally relevant teaching looks like. As our time working together became more consistent, the comfort level Alicia felt in using her voice increased. Our dyad partnership informed our professional relationship, giving us the opportunity for a mutual collegial relationship as learners together. There were multiple things we did to learn to be learners together, including:

- co-mentoring and shared learning;
- formal and informal classroom visits;
- intentional and direct language about classroom visits;
- difficult conversations.

An issue that could have potentially hindered co-mentoring was our positioning as administrator and teacher. Alicia describes how it was difficult at first to see Bilal as anything other than her administrator, particularly because during their time as a dyad he was her supervising assistant principal. To alleviate this power dynamic, Bilal challenged Alicia to take risks in the classroom without the underlying intimidation of having a formal observation and a write-up. Alicia explained that Bilal would clarify the distinctions of his classroom visits. He would come into the classroom to learn from Alicia as she explored and tried new practices. Although he provided feedback, he worked to avoid a judgmental eye. At other times, he was in the classroom to provide more evaluative notes on her teaching and what he learned. This approach and practice allowed Alicia to feel at ease in the relationship. Once this comfort level was established, she started feeling as if it really was a co-mentorship. Alicia invited Bilal to her classroom on a regular basis, excited to share the work the students were doing and sometimes not realizing how amazing it really was until he pointed it out to her. At the same time, Bilal learned from Alicia as he saw culturally relevant pedagogies in practice and learned from Alicia's strong stance in terms of supporting her students' needs to address issues of injustice (discussed later in this chapter).

We also found that tough conversations helped foster a working relationship that was collegial, centered in mutual respect, and not based on the traditional hierarchy between teacher and administrator. Discussions about race and the relationships between Black males and police officers brought on by events like the murders of Michael Brown, Alton Sterling, and Eric Garner forced us to work hard to establish a relationship based on trust, patience, candor, and honesty. For Alicia, as Latina married to a White, New York City police officer, and Bilal, as an African Latino man who identifies as Black, this meant that we had some discussing to do.

Bilal initiated an initial discussion by asking Alicia if they could talk about the recent events of Black men murdered at the hands of police officers. Bilal's curiosity was centered in wondering about Alicia's perspective as the wife of a White New York City Police officer. Bilal explained that the tension between police officers and African American males was not a new experience. He shared how some of his own interactions with police officers as a young boy and into manhood were often contentious, because many White police officers had not confronted their biases when it came to interacting with young men of Color, particularly African American males. The constant reminder of how Black men and men of Color were mistreated by law enforcement officers in the United States of America would not allow Bilal to avoid this opportunity to share and learn with Alicia. He knew that, as a White police officer's wife, Alicia might be defensive and that she would think her husband would be under attack. Bilal initially hesitated because he did not want to create discomfort in their working relationship. Alicia was equally hesitant, feeling great concern for her husband particularly in the wake of the killing of two White police officers in his jurisdiction. It was the importance of the topic and the urgent obligation to make a connection that led us to persevere in deepening our relationship. Because we took the time to hear each other's views, we grew as colleagues, practitioners, and co-learners. As co-mentors, we looked to explore, grow, and share what we learned from our own lives and the lives of students and families. In this way, our dyad partnership actualized principles underpinning culturally relevant, responsive, and sustaining pedagogies.

Culturally Relevant, Responsive, and Sustaining Teaching in Alicia's Classroom

With this background, we learned together as teacher and administrator about how culturally relevant, responsive, and sustaining teaching influenced students' literacy growth in Alicia's second-grade classroom. Using practitioner inquiry and action research methodologies (Mills & Butroyd, 2014), we collected data focused on our daily discussions of students' responses to Alicia's teaching and as we documented the teaching itself. In the process, we nurtured our relationship as a dyad and our growing understandings about culturally relevant curriculum. This section highlights five instructional opportunities that illustrate culturally relevant, responsive, and sustaining teaching as we have come to understand each concept.

Opening-Day Writing: Cultural Responsiveness in Action

If you walked into Alicia Boardman's second-grade bilingual class on any given day, you would see 24 students engaged in learning centered in culturally relevant, responsive, and sustaining pedagogy. One particular day, students were using morning meeting as a time to debate a topic that was very important to them: *Who was the best baseball team in New York?* New York is home to two major league baseball teams, the New York Yankees and The Mets. Of course, there is always a rivalry that begins as baseball season starts. The children were enjoying a very friendly discussion about which team was the best, and Alicia enjoyed the back-and-forth banter from the students. Alicia decided to use this as a learning experience, taking into consideration the New York State standards that required students to write persuasive essays. Alicia's students offered the following excited thoughts during that first discussion in morning meeting:

> The Mets are the best team! My Mami and Papi love them too!
>
> ¡A mi no me gusta los Mets … . me gusta los Yankees!/I do not like the Mets, I like the Yankees!
>
> The Yankees are the best team! I love watching them on TV!
>
> Tomorrow I am going to wear my Yankees shirt!
>
> ¡A mi tambien me gusta los Yankees. Pero a mi hermano, no le gusta ninguno!/ I also like the Yankees. But my brother doesn't like either team!

After the initial discussion, Alicia took time doing her own research on the two teams. Alicia used the Internet and televised documentaries to expand her knowledge of the teams. She then asked students to research their favorite teams. In order to make sure students had independent readings for their research based on their instructional reading level, Alicia created many of the reading materials herself. Alicia conducted online research and perused library stacks to collect images and information about the two different teams. With this collection of pictures and information, Alicia created personalized and authentic reading materials for her students. After reading the texts, students completed a graphic organizer comparing the two teams. Then, they began writing notes about their writing, noting the important reasons why their particular team was the "best" in New York. The students knew that the purpose of their writing was to convince their classmates that their team was better. Except Aliya. Aliya was not a baseball fan. She was not interested in the topic of baseball. According to Aliya, her family was not interested in baseball either. She said, "I do not have a favorite team. So I am just going to talk to everyone else and then decide which team is the best." Alicia wanted Aliya to feel included in this class activity and be as engaged and motivated as the other students. She told Aliya to speak to the other students and decide if there was a team that she felt she wanted to learn more about. The other students were excited and anxious to be able to convince a classmate to "join their side." This opportunity for choice gave Aliya agency to learn why each baseball team was important to her classmates. In this way, Alicia foregrounded students' own everyday linguistic and cultural practices (Gutiérrez & Johnson, 2017; Paris & Alim, 2017; Vasquez, 2004). The final writing piece was showcased on lined paper with their corresponding team logo (Figure 4.3).

This opening writing activity, like most of the practices in Alicia's class, became about more than just baseball. It became an opportunity for students to build their language skills through informal discussion, which is vital for

FIGURE 4.3 My Favorite Team writing document templates.

emergent bilingual students. Likewise, providing a variety of tasks and encouraging personal participation in the decision making created a learning environment grounded in "choice and authenticity," exemplifying what Gay (2010) termed "culturally responsive teaching praxis" (pp. 215–224). This approach demonstrated cultural responsiveness as Alicia learned about and responded to students' interests and strengths to build engaging curriculum (Gay, 2010) and simultaneously met state and national standards. The discussions and arguments generated during this opening-day writing project allowed students to create content that they cared about and work with a sense of pride that fostered a refined and quality product, a central goal of culturally responsive teaching (Gay, 2010). Through this writing project, the heritage and contemporary practices of students and their families and their communities were valued and leveraged.

Building a Culturally Relevant Classroom Library

Culturally relevant teaching focuses on fostering academic achievement, cultural competence, and sociopolitical consciousness to "develop students who can both understand and critique the existing social order" (Ladson-Billings, 1995, p. 474). One way that Alicia addressed the second tenet—developing cultural competence—was by building a richly diverse classroom library. After attending the 2013 National Conference Teachers of English annual convention in Boston, Massachusetts, Alicia's vision of a classroom library changed. At the time, it consisted of books that she inherited from previous teachers and classrooms. Following conference discussions about texts that created both windows and mirrors for students (Bishop, 1990), Alicia began to put more thought into her classroom library. In essence, Alicia committed to creating a classroom book collection that would "transcend the negative effects of the dominant culture" (Ladson-Billings, 1994, p. 17) as the only or primary representation in her library. She realized that a culturally relevant library must feature authors, illustrators, and characters of Color represented richly, not tokenized. Her library at that time did not. So, Alicia spent time researching authors of Color, as well as books that featured characters of Color in a positive light (see Table 4.1 for resources for creating a culturally relevant classroom library).

TABLE 4.1 Resources for creating a culturally relevant classroom library.

#We Need Diverse Books: https://diversebooks.org/resources/where-to-find-diverse-books/
Center for the Study of Multicultural Children's Literature: https://www.csmcl.org/
Kitaab World: https://kitaabworld.com/
Latinos in Kid Lit: https://latinosinkidlit.com/
Diverse Book Finder: https://diversebookfinder.org/
Social Justice Books: https://socialjusticebooks.org/

Alicia learned about authors like Jacqueline Woodson, Christopher Meyers, Matt De La Peña, Monica Brown, and Meg Medina among many others. Once she made a list of new culturally relevant and authentic titles that she wanted to include, she used the website www.donorschoose.org to create a wishlist of books, with the hope that others would donate so she would be able to make this purchase. Her request for books was quickly fulfilled, and her culturally relevant classroom library began to grow. It's important to note that Alicia knew merely "adding some books about People of Color, having a classroom Kwanzaa celebration, or posting 'diverse' images" (Ladson-Billings, 2014, p. 82) did not make her classroom culturally relevant. She had to be intentional about incorporating and maintaining students' cultures in all aspects of instruction and curriculum, starting with her book collection.

As time went on, Alicia has realized the impact of the diverse library on students' academic growth. Students were more motivated to read because they were excited to see themselves and their languages reflected in the books in their classroom, and engage with the books in ways that helped them challenge and critique problematic aspects of their world (discussed further in the next example) (Bishop, 1990; Souto-Manning, 2013). Creating a culturally relevant library with diverse books has become and continues to be Alicia's passion, and she continues working to ensure that her students have a library that fosters their knowledge of self and culture (Figure 4.4).

FIGURE 4.4 Culturally relevant classroom library of diverse and multicultural books.

The Celia Cruz and Tito Puente Project

One day, Alicia heard a student talking about how someone called her mother "bad" because of the dark color of her skin. Recognizing the issue of colorism (bias based on the darkness of skin color), Alicia was determined to find children's books to showcase the beauty of dark-skinned Latinas. Alicia looked through her now extensive diverse classroom library and found the book *Me llama Celia/My name is Celia* by Monica Brown (2004) about the famous Afro-Cuban singer often called the Queen of Salsa. Alicia read the book aloud to her students, stopping to admire and discuss the bright, beautiful illustrations, words that sounded like lyrics to a song, rich dialogue, and Celia's beautiful skin.

Engaging with this book, the students also learned of the importance of Celia's famous phrase *AZUCAR!* (Sugar!). The children loved that the phrase connected to her homeland of Cuba, where sugar has been grown for centuries. It reminded some of the children of their families' homelands and languages or specific words that connected them to those places. They learned about the injustices Celia Cruz faced, and how she immigrated to Mexico and then the United States to escape the dictatorship of Fidel Castro. Many students linked Celia's story of immigration to their own stories of traveling (most from Central America) to the United States. They began asking questions about Celia, salsa music, and Cuba. After they finished the story, Alicia and her students watched videos of Celia performing and were able to hear her using her famous phrase *AZUCAR!* The children commented in awe of the sounds of the instruments, her beautiful skin, and her bright colored hair and clothing. They were excited to listen to the music spoken in Spanish much like their own home languages. As they listened to the salsa music and watched how she danced, students began to connect Celia's moves to a variety of their favorite artists, such as Selena Gomez, Beyoncé, Romeo, Daddy Yankee, Jennifer Lopez, and Ariana Grande—without Alicia's prompting or help.

The students also learned how Celia, although she was a Latina, faced racism in Cuba because she was Afro Latina. Students were particularly intrigued by a line in the book that read, "Some people would not let me sing in their contests because of the color of my skin" (Brown, 2004, n.p.). This started discussions around racism and colorism and what they called "being treated fairly." They had all recently learned about Rosa Parks, and were able to make connections between racism in the Jim Crow South and Celia's similar experiences in Cuba. They made connections to acts of injustice today, and their own experiences with discrimination as immigrants. It made students feel as if their own experiences were validated and real. This connected them even more to the story, and more importantly to Celia.

When students left school after the first day of being exposed to Celia Cruz, they were excited to share with their families. Alicia instructed students to ask their parents if they had any information about Celia Cruz to share with them. In this way, families continued the discussions at home as family members shared stories of their own exposure to salsa music, but also to discrimination. As one child reported the next day: "This reminds me of when someone said my Mami was bad because she was dark skinned. They were from Honduras like us."

Alicia also introduced another book by Monica Brown, *Tito Puente, Mambo King/Rey del Mambo* (Brown, 2013). She introduced Tito's music and the students were excited to learn about his collaboration with Celia Cruz. Since students were enamored with both Celia and Tito, Alicia built a unit of study within her writing curriculum around them. They first spent time comparing the two musicians using a Venn diagram, and then used this graphic organizer to construct an informational essay. As the days went on, Alicia played the music of Celia and Tito every day during writers' workshop. Students treated the unit of study on Celia Cruz and Tito Puente with the same sense of joy as they did their "free time"—they engaged voluntarily and enthusiastically. Students demonstrated and learned the salsa dances they saw Celia doing, and commented that they would go home and ask their families to play Cruz or Puente music and dance while they did their homework or played. Students exclaimed: "My mom loves Celia Cruz! She told me all about her when I got home" and "The music makes me happy! I love writing and hearing the music at the same time."

The Celia Cruz and Tito Puente project allowed Alicia's students to celebrate their heritage language, skin tone, and honor their cultural history and knowledge. The students engaged with books, watched videos, listened to music, demonstrated and taught dances, and wrote informational essays to share that they were learning. Through this work, major tenets of culturally relevant and responsive teaching were captured as students developed cultural competence and a critical consciousness through Alicia's responsiveness to their culturally driven interests. Together they discussed oppression against Afro Latinas, embracing tenets of culturally sustaining teaching as they forefronted multilingual multicultural heritage and historicized texts to link past and present (Alim & Paris, 2017).

The Maya Angelou Project

On May 28th, 2014, Maya Angelou passed away. Alicia had grown up watching Dr. Angelou on television, reading her poetry, and had always being intrigued and mesmerized by her voice. Walking into her classroom following the news of Angelou's passing, Alicia was sure she wanted to expose her students to this poet and her poetry so that they could have the privilege of learning more about her. During morning meeting, she discussed with them who Maya Angelou was and asked students if they had ever heard of her. They did not know who she was, so Alicia began by reading to them some of Angelou's poetry. The students asked many questions. They were intrigued with the fact that Angelou was a poet, and wanted to learn more about her. Many of the questions students had were things that Alicia did not have the answers to, such as Maya Angelou's birth place and her motivation to write. They researched the questions together, using the classroom computers and whiteboard. Alicia then found YouTube videos of interviews of Maya Angelou. She told students to close their eyes while they listened to her voice. Then the students described her: "She has a soft voice, like my grandma" and "It sounds like she is singing," and "Her voice feels soft, like a cloud."

Alicia searched for an Angelou poem that students would be able to connect with. Most of her students were new to the United States and many had difficult experiences immigrating to New York from Central America. For this reason, Alicia read the poem "Life Doesn't Frighten Me" (Angelou, 1994). Students spent a lot of time listening to the poem being read by both Alicia and Maya Angelou. Alicia spent some time discussing with the class things that frightened them. It started with things like dark rooms, loud noises, and scary movies. Becoming more engaged, they discussed fears such as being separated from family members, or walking alone. The students were then given the poem with parts of it missing, so they were able to "write" the poem with their own fears, in Spanish or English. Students discussed how these fears were going to make them stronger, and how they were not going to allow those fears to dominate them. In this way, Dr. Angelou's message empowered students to create creative writing in new linguistically and culturally dexterous ways (Paris & Alim, 2014, p. 91), in order to identify their oral and written poetic voice.

Si, Somos Latinos

For many years, Alicia had assisted in organizing the school's Hispanic Heritage month celebration, which involved students creating a museum of special artifacts from home. However, through her study of culturally relevant teaching, she wanted to go beyond a "heroes and holidays" approach. This is why Alicia introduced the students to the text *¡Si! Somos Latinos* by Alma Flor Ada and Isabel Campo (2014). Although the text is labeled as a level "U," which is well above the suggested second-grade reading level, Alicia used and amplified the text in ways that assisted students in understanding and analyzing it. She used English and Spanish versions of the book to engage students in discussions about their families, home countries, and heritage languages. Alicia's focus and intention was to work toward the reclamation of her students' and their families' histories, contributions, and possibilities of cultural communities. She wanted the students to be proud of their Latinx culture, so she foregrounded their heritage and their families within the curriculum (Gutiérrez & Johnson, 2017).

¡Si! Somos Latinos sparked conversations with the students about the different Latin American countries that were represented within their own classroom and school. They discussed how they were all Latinos, despite the fact that they came from different countries in Latin America and that some spoke more fluent Spanish than others. The students went home that evening and interviewed their families. They asked them about the countries their parents, grandparents, and other family members were from. Some students returned to class the next day

excited to announce that their entire family was from El Salvador, while others were proud to share that their family came from many Latin American countries. Because of her commitment to honoring the students' cultures, she fostered a humanizing community within her classroom, recognizing that the traditions of her students and their families were sacred to them and extended across several generations.

The students used the information given to them by their families to write their own pages for a classroom Si, Somos Latinos book. Alicia created a document for them to use as a template that mirrored a section in the book:

> Me Llamo _________
> Soy de ____________________
>
> ___________________________________
>
> Yo Soy Latino

The Si, Somos Latinos engagement allowed the students to connect with heritage language via academic activity that had meaning to their families and their culture (Ladson-Billings, 1995). Alicia's willingness to pay attention and respond to students' evolving interests and ideas, allowing this practice to inform instruction, epitomizes features of culturally relevant, responsive, and sustaining pedagogies particularly as she moved beyond viewing heritage, cultural, and community practices as resources to be considered only during certain times of the year to making them intrinsic to day-to-day classroom life.

Next Steps: Sustaining the Work Institutionally

An important aspect of this work is its sustaining institutional impact. Our mutual mentorship supported Bilal's abilities to build from Alicia's classroom work and from the courage of her convictions to work with his leadership team to create ongoing schoolwide professional development to begin building an educational institution grounded in the tenets of culturally responsive, culturally relevant, and ultimately, culturally sustaining teaching. One of the first steps in our efforts to use the work to impact practice was to co-author a peer-reviewed journal article, "Engaging Children and Families in Culturally Relevant Literacies," published in the *Journal of Family Strengths* (Piña, Nash, Boardman, Polson, & Panther, 2015). In addition, since 2013, Alicia and Bilal have shared their work at regional and national conferences, hosted Twitter chats, produced webinars, and published writing related to the vision and practice of culturally relevant teaching. Alicia has co-authored a peer-reviewed journal article, "La Historia de Mi Nombre: A Culturally Sustaining Early Literacy Practice," published in *The Reading Teacher* (Nash, Panther, & Arce-Boardman, 2018). She also participated as co-author of the highly celebrated book *No More Culturally Irrelevant Teaching* (Souto-Manning, Llerena, Martell, Maguire, & Arce-Boardman, 2018). Additionally, Alicia was selected to serve as an officer for the Equity through Excellence in Education initiative in the Uniondale School District.

As assistant principal, Bilal facilitated student-led community marches and peace rallies. Later, when Bilal became principal of the school, he began highlighting the importance of articulating a clear vision to the whole school community that Northern Parkway School honors the language, the history, and the culture of all the students and their families. This particular message of cultural relevance and responsiveness is sustained by including this messaging and vision in family letters, postings on the school website, and expressing this mission publicly as often as possible. In addition, Bilal and his school leadership team of building administrators, teachers, and parent–teacher association have worked together to identify customized programming and formal presentations to meet the needs of the students and vision of the school.

Strategies, Outcomes, Legacies

Paris and Alim (2017) explained that "culturally sustaining educators connect present learning to the histories of racial, ethnic, and linguistic communities, to the histories of neighborhoods and cities, and the histories of the larger states and nation-states that they are part of" (p. 6). The work generated by Alicia (Table 4.2) did just that as she celebrated the children's home and heritage languages and helped them embrace their rich heritages in conjunction with their own learning.

The positive outcomes from this work are evidenced throughout this chapter but also in conventional assessments. Figure 4.5 showcases norm-referenced data via the Fountas and Pinnell benchmark assessment of oral reading fluency and comprehension (2010) from fall, winter, and spring of six of Alicia's students. These scores highlight student growth in reading comprehension and fluency, with almost all children surpassing the second-grade target of reading at level "N."

Our work demonstrates how children can—and must—grow academically without losing or denying their languages, literacies, cultures, and histories (Alim & Paris, 2017). Through learning together, we have not only impacted students in Alicia's classroom and other teachers within and beyond Northern Parkway School, but have formed a long-lasting, supportive, co-mentoring collegial relationship.

We are inspired by Maya Angelou's words, "There is no greater agony than bearing an untold story inside you" from Angelou's (1997) autobiography *I Know Why the Caged Bird Sings*. We feel they speak to the way we strove to tap into the untold stories of students in Alicia's classroom. We hope our work inspires other educators to mine the untold stories of the children, families, and communities that you serve and to use their brilliance to institute policies and practices that insist on the institutionalization of rich, vibrant, multilingual, multicultural educational experiences in the lives of every child.

TABLE 4.2 Culturally relevant, culturally responsive, and culturally sustaining instructional strategies/descriptions in Alicia's classroom.

Strategy	*Description*
Morning Meeting	Morning meeting creates a classroom space for conversations based on student voices, interests, world events, and the like.
Student-Led Writing	Building writing units that are required or mandated (e.g., persuasive essays) can easily be connected to students' strengths, cultures, languages.
Original Reading Materials	When it is challenging to find age-appropriate reading materials on a certain topic, do your own research and create the reading materials. The benefit of this is students have age-appropriate materials and this is authentic and original.
Multimedia Resources	Playing music, videos, and using the whiteboard interactively connects students to the topic in an engaging way.
Post-it Notes	Use post-its for students to write notes as they are reading a text. These notes eventually are used to construct an extended response on the reading.
Pictures as Tools to Save Data	Take pictures of work that students do, so that you are able to reference them in the future. This allows the students to reference the photographs for their writing.
Historical Figures	Inquiry about historical figures like Maya Angelou, Tito Puente, and Celia Cruz allowed students to make connections with current figures such as Jennifer Lopez, Romeo, Beyonce among many others.
Diverse Classroom Libraries	Classroom libraries feature various authors and characters of different races, cultures and religions in texts that are written and illustrated by members of the group addressed in the texts. Students are able to see themselves and their families in the classroom and more engaged and motivated. This also allows them to have a voice in their learning

Student	*September*	*February*	*May*
Dallana	M	N	N+
Steven	L	N	N+
Jackie	J	K	M
Emerson	H	K	N
Jeffrey	C	E	J
Frineth	C	E	G

FIGURE 4.5 Alicia's students' fall, winter, and spring literacy data.

References

Alim, H. S., & Paris, D. (2017). What is culturally sustaining pedagogy and why does it matter? In D. Paris & H. S. Alim (Eds.), *Culturally sustaining pedagogies: Teaching and learning for justice in a changing world* (pp. 1–24). New York, NY: Teachers College Press.

Angelou, M. (1994). *Wouldn't take nothing for my journey now*. New York, NY: Bantam Books.

Angelou, M. (1997). *I know why the caged bird sings*. New York, NY: Bantam.

Bishop, R. S. (1990). Mirrors, windows, and sliding glass doors. *Perspectives*, 6(3), ix–xi. Retrieved from https://scenicregional.org/wp-content/uploads/2017/08/Mirrors-Windows-and-Sliding-Glass-Doors.pdf

Bomer, K. (2010). *Hidden gems. Naming and teaching from the brilliance in every student's writing*. Portsmouth, NH: Heinemann.

Brice-Heath, S., & Mangiola, L. (1991). *Children of promise: Literate activity in linguistically and culturally diverse classrooms*. NEA School Restructuring Series. West Haven, CT: National Education Association.

Campano, G. (2007). *Immigrant students and literacy: Reading, writing, and remembering*. New York, NY: Teachers College Press.

Darder, A. (1991). *Culture and power in the classroom: A critical foundation for bicultural education*. Westport, CT: Greenwood Publishing Group.

Gates Jr, Henry Louis (2011). *Black in Latin America*. New York, NY: New York University Press.

Gay, G. (2010). *Culturally responsive teaching: Theory, research, and practice*. New York, NY: Teachers College Press.

Gutiérrez, K. D., Baquedano-López, P., & Tejada, C. (1999). Rethinking diversity: Hybridity and hybrid language practices in third space. *Mind, Culture, and Activity*, 6, 286–303.

Gutiérrez, K. D., & Johnson, P. (2017). Understanding identity sampling and cultural repertoires: Advancing learning in justice pedagogies. In D. Paris & H. S. Alim (Eds.), *Culturally sustaining pedagogies: Teaching and learning for justice in a changing world* (pp. 247–260). New York, NY: Teachers College Press.

Ladson-Billings, G. (1994). *The dreamkeepers: Successful teachers of African-American children*. San Francisco, CA: Jossey-Bass.

Ladson-Billings, G. (1995). But that's just good teaching! The case for culturally relevant pedagogy. *Theory into Practice*, 34, 159–165.

Ladson-Billings, G. (2014). Culturally relevant pedagogy 2.0: a.k.a. the remix. *Harvard Educational Review*, 84, 74–84.

Mills, G. E. (2011). *Action research: A guide for the teacher researcher*. New York, NY: Pearson.

Mills, G. E., & Butroyd, R. (2014). *Action research: A guide for the teacher researcher*. Boston, MA: Pearson.

Nash, K. T., Panther, L. & Arce-Boardman, A. (2018). La historia de mi nombre: A culturally sustaining early literacy practice. *The Reading Teacher*, 71, 605–609.

Paris, D., & Alim, H. S. (2014). What are we seeking to sustain through culturally sustaining pedagogy? A loving critique forward. *Harvard Educational Review*, 84, 85–100.

Paris, D., & Alim, H. S. (2017). *Culturally sustaining pedagogies: Teaching and learning for justice in a changing world*. New York, NY: Teachers College Press.

Piña, P., Nash, K. T., Boardman, A., Polson, B., & Panther, L. (2015). Engaging children and families in culturally relevant literacies. *Journal of Family Strengths*, 15(2), article 3.

Souto-Manning, M. (2013). *Multicultural teaching in the early childhood classroom: Approaches, strategies, and tools, preschool-2nd grade*. New York, NY: Teachers College Press.

Souto-Manning, M., Llerena, C., Martell, J., Maguire, A., & Arce-Boardman, A. (2018) *No more culturally irrelevant teaching*. Portsmouth, NH: Heinemann.

Vans Ausdale, D., & Feagin, J. *The first R: How children learn race and racism*. New York, NY: Rowman & Little Publishers.

Vasquez, V. (2004). *Literacy as social practice; primary voices k-6: Community, choice and content in urban classroom*. Urbana, IL: National Council of Teachers of English.

Children's Literature Cited

Ada, A. F., & Campoy, I. (2014). *¡Si! Somos Latinos*. Madrid: Alfaguara.

Brown, M. (2004). *My name is Celia/Me llama Celia: The life of Celiz Cruz/La vida de Celia Cruz*. New York, NY: HarperCollins.

Brown, M. (2013). *Tito Puente, mambo king/rey del mambo*. New York, NY: HarperCollins.

5

GROWING OUR VILLAGE

The Power of Shared Knowledge in Early Childhood Literacy

Crystal Glover and Chinyere Harris

> It makes me feel good and proud when you talk about Mexico because Mexico really does have a big heart and they work really hard. I like it when we can speak in Spanish and English... and when you gave us homework about the Day of the Dead, that meant really nice to me... it shows me that you really do care about Mexico and it made me want to do my homework!
>
> ~ *Second-grade Latina student in Chinyere's class*

An array of plastic elementary school-sized chairs lined the perimeter of Chinyere Harris's second-grade classroom on a cold November morning. Some chairs were tall, some short and wobbly, some blue, others bright red or faded yellow, but all were filled with proud parents awaiting the cultural celebration that would soon begin. The children in the class, primed and ready to present the projects on which they had worked earnestly for the past few weeks, peeked back at their parents and family members, some offering a short wave and others unable to withstand the urge to jump up and get a quick hug or kiss.

To anyone who entered her classroom, it became instantly clear how much Chinyere's students love being there. And after spending a few minutes in Chinyere's room, it was easy to see why children are attracted to this bright, colorful, and engaging space. On most days, music played softly in the background of the classroom. The music varied from Spanish, to Indian, K-Pop, and classical. Children were exposed to a variety of musical genres and genuinely seemed to appreciate them all. Music was a part of the relaxed and welcoming climate and it immediately draws you into the room.

Throughout the typical school day, children found individual or group spaces around the room in which to complete their work. While a few children opted to work at the desks, most took an individual mat or gathered in pairs or groups on small rugs around the room. There was always a soft murmur of chatter in the room, but this didn't seem to interfere with those children who elected to work independently. In most cases, children were so engaged in their own work that they barely seemed to notice what the others are doing.

On this particular day, as more parents arrived to the now standing-room-only space, some began to converse in Spanish while others, whose home and heritage languages included Urdu, Russian, and French, looked on with anticipation about the upcoming student presentations that would offer a glimpse into the histories, customs, and beliefs that they had been unable to share with others since arriving in America. Just before 10:30 a.m. Chinyere made her way to the front of the room to give a warm welcome and thank the parents for their presence and support on the projects the children had prepared to share. After a round of applause from the parents, children took their turns and enlightened the audience on a family tradition, practice, picture, or artifact. Over the next 45 minutes, Chinyere's second-grade classroom transformed from an instructional space into a community of learners, friends, and family. Children and adults alike witnessed examples of the children's efforts to illustrate through their work that "[i]t is not our differences that divide us. It is our inability to recognize, accept, and celebrate those differences" (Lorde, 1986, p. 22).

An Introduction to Our Work

The fall of 2013 was a year of new beginnings. Chinyere Harris was beginning her first year as a classroom teacher and Crystal Glover was embarking upon a new career as an early childhood teacher educator. We were both overjoyed about our new careers and eager to make an impact in our respective fields. Having previously worked together on a research project when Chinyere was a Master's student and Crystal was a doctoral student, we shared a common interest in learning more about culturally relevant pedagogy and were committed to sharing our passion for teaching and learning in ways that honor and value children as cultural beings.

This chapter describes elements of our journey as we set out to develop, implement, document, and study the impact of culturally relevant early literacy practices in an ethnically, racially, and linguistically diverse, urban elementary school in Charlotte, North Carolina. What began as an earnest classroom investigation using constructivist grounded theory methods (Charmaz, 2014) blossomed into a complex and courageous campaign to infuse culturally relevant literacy strategies school-wide which we see as critical to being able to sustain the work and the students' cultures and languages. When student achievement improved as a result of our work, so did the interests and curiosities of administrators, teachers, and parents at the school. Ultimately, we extended our work to include a committee of concerned stakeholders made up of educators, families, and community leaders whose efforts to promote culturally relevant and sustaining pedagogy became an authentic representation of the notion that it takes a village to raise a child.

After completing our two years together and revisiting data from Chinyere's classroom, we realized that our work could not merely focus on culturally relevant teaching for a moment in time but had to be conceptualized as to how it might affect long-lasting change in our own teaching and in the systems in which we work. It was and is about figuring out ways to overturn and replace the ubiquitous White Gaze (Morrison, 1998) that has served to misrepresent or invisibilize the strengths of children of Color. This chapter portrays many of our moments of enlightenment and discovery as well as pitfalls and successes as we studied together, generated teaching practices, and broadened each other's perspectives. This chapter outlines a few of our attempts to "import multiculturalism and multilingualism [into early literacy instruction in ways that] disrupt dominant narratives that superficially affirm differences and diversities while maintaining the status quo" (Kinloch, 2017, p. 28).

Establishing the Village: Meet the Authors

As women of Color in education, we discovered many similarities in our mutual commitment to educational attainment. However, as outlined in our introductions below, the beginning of our own educational journeys stood in stark contrast to one another. Despite the differences in educational experiences, we were both drawn to the principles of culturally relevant and later culturally sustaining teaching and saw both as integral to our work as leaders and learners. Together,

FIGURE 5.1 Chinyere Harris.

we embarked on a new journey as a dyad in the first cohort of the professional dyads and culturally relevant teaching (PDCRT).

Chinyere

Chinyere identifies as a woman of Color whose mother is African American and specializes in geriatrics and whose father who is Nigerian having come to the United States to earn his Ph.D. in chemistry. Chinyere grew up in Charlotte, North Carolina where she and her sister attended a majority White private school. She grew up in a family who understood the importance and implications of a culturally and politically comprehensive education. They also ensured that Chinyere understood how to use her knowledge and privilege to evaluate and act against systemic bias in critically conscious ways. Chinyere's family ensured that she understood that she must use her opportunity and position to secure equity and equality for those for whom it has been denied.

Chinyere frequently shares narratives and examples from her own life with her students about what it was like growing up as a person who is African American and Nigerian. Chinyere and her students often shared their experiences about the social dichotomies that existed in their classroom and communities. In one particular conversation, an African American male student called a female student from West Africa "black" during their literacy class. His tone implied that being "black" was bad. When Chinyere asked the male student if he realized that both he and his classmate were the same skin complexion, he had no response. He was asked to think about his words. The in-class discussion that ensued focused on why at times African American Blacks and Africans can be pitted against each other even when they are both "Othered" (Mohanty, 2000) by members of the dominant culture. Instead of being ignored or deemed inappropriate, these types of narratives become a part of the curriculum in Chinyere's classroom.

At the time of this work, Chinyere worked as a teacher in the second and fourth grades, while earning a Master's degree in Education focused on Teaching English as a Second Language. As a second- and fourth-grade teacher, Chinyere was able to engage with bright, caring, and intelligent learners and their families. She was not only fortunate to learn from them and be a part of a rich community of individuals, but she was also able to acknowledge and honor their stories as legitimate elements of her literacy program and curriculum. Chinyere was passionate about engaging and facilitating learning with students and families. She worked to construct curriculum that allowed students to see themselves, their communities, and their culture as foundationally significant in the history of the world. Chinyere is currently a primary teacher at the School at Columbia University and is pursuing doctoral studies in Curriculum and Teaching at Teachers College, Columbia University in New York City. She brings her core educational philosophies into the instruction she provides her students and into her own research.

FIGURE 5.2 Crystal P. Glover.

Crystal

Crystal Polite Glover is an African American Assistant Professor of Early Childhood Education at Winthrop University in Rock Hill, South Carolina. A first-generation college graduate, she grew up as the only child of a single, working-class mother and attended public schools in the same small, southeastern city where her family had lived for several generations. As an only child, Crystal grew up an avid reader. She rarely left home without a book and almost always returned home from any outing with a new book to add to her collection. Although enjoyable and engaging, most of the books that Crystal read as a young girl were devoid of characters that looked like her. As her reading interests grew more diverse, Crystal began to notice that all of the novels she read focused on White children and White families going about life in their all-White worlds. Though she lacked the terminology to define her conundrum, Crystal was experiencing the impact of the ever-present White Gaze (Morrison, 1998) in literature, which portrays Whiteness as the standard to which people of all other backgrounds are held. When books represent exclusively White ways of doing and being, children of Color are denied opportunities to identify with their own "rich and innovative linguistic, literate, and cultural practices" (Paris & Alim, 2014, p. 86). Ironically, this White Gaze would later come to characterize and frame Crystal's academic and professional experiences for many years to come as she was forced to defend her African American narrative amid her primarily White peers in classroom discussions or faculty forums.

Crystal began her career as an early childhood teacher in a small community school filled with children of Color and emerging bi/multilinguals. She sought to intentionally infuse culturally relevant practices into her instruction and to build meaningful relationships with the students and families in her reach. Later, Crystal extended this reach by working with preservice and practicing teachers to decolonize education and design curriculum intending to "sustain revitalize, and nurture the identities, practices, ingenuity, agency, and humanity of youth of Color, on their terms" (Dominguez, 2017, p. 226). Crystal's experiences working as a dyad member in the first cohort of PDCRT strengthened her journey to becoming a culturally relevant teacher educator in ways she had never imagined.

A Framework for Our Work Together

In this section, we describe ways we worked together as co-researchers and co-learners. We outline the procedures we used to select our rich and varied data sources and we detail the ways in which we came to develop and process the information we collected. Our ideas, interactions, and instruction were all immersed in and informed by culturally relevant pedagogy. As we navigated our journey together, we discovered new developments and ideas of culturally sustaining pedagogies which also began to influence our work. These newly defined pedagogies carved a different path in our journey that led to contemporary interpretations of the culturally relevant practices we embraced during our initial implementations of the project.

Establishing New Spring Elementary School as the Village Home

At the time of our work together, Chinyere taught at New Spring Elementary (pseudonym), a large, diverse K–5 school in Charlotte, North Carolina. There were approximately 800 learners in 24 classrooms at this neighborhood, Title I school. New Spring was located in a working-class community not far from the university where we both attended graduate school. Ninety-two percent of learners within the school received free and reduced lunch. Forty-seven percent of learners were Latinx, 39% were African American, 5% were listed as White, and 8% were listed as "other." We engaged with learners at New Spring who spoke: French, Igbo, Urdu, Russian, and Spanish.

New Spring is part of a large, urban school district where mandates regarding literacy instruction were rampant. Teachers in the district were expected to follow a structured literacy curriculum and to assess student performance using standardized assessment measures. We knew that the work within our dyad would have to involve district-mandated literacy materials and assessments, but we also committed to supplementing our instruction and assessment with books, articles, films, websites, commercials, and blogs beyond the mainstream materials. We also sought to serve as inspiration to other teachers who had grown weary of mainstream materials. We worked with literacy facilitators and coaches to ensure that our goals met school requirements. New Spring became our village home.

At the beginning of the project, we met weekly to discuss shared professional readings and unpack our work in Chinyere's classroom. These meetings lasted approximately two hours and typically preceded the one day a week that Crystal came to the classroom. This was an iterative process as school-wide changes to the literacy schedule impacted our plan for literacy instruction. Recognizing that schedule change is the norm for many teachers, we did not let any administrative changes interrupt or close down our planning and persevered to discuss and generate culturally relevant strategies that we hoped would allow the children of Color and emerging bi/multilingual children in Chinyere's class to bring their cultural and linguistic experience to the forefront. On the days that Crystal came to the classroom, we worked together with the children to implement our plans. To be clear, our work was not limited to the days that Crystal visited the classroom. It was continuously and intentionally woven throughout all of our interactions with the children and their families. Our charge extended to homework assignments, phone calls with parents, and even field trips. We made the tenets of culturally relevant pedagogy the well from which we drew our essential knowledge in our work at New Spring.

Documenting Our Work

As part of our journey, we interviewed students and their families and video-recorded class sessions and special events. We also took detailed notes of classroom interactions involving culturally relevant and sustaining practice and we documented student performance using observation checklists. In addition, we collected student work samples and assessment data such as beginning, middle, and end of the year literacy comprehension levels. We chose each of the information sources for its unique and descriptive qualities. For example, sources such as the interviews with students and parents offered individual perspectives on our work, while the observation checklists presented a more holistic view of the impact our instruction was having on students. As time went on, we expanded our work to include other educators. To document this part of our work, we collected survey data from all of the teachers within the school. The goal of the surveys was to record changes in thought and action among teachers within the school following professional development and other investigative experiences with culturally relevant pedagogy.

Insights: Our Dyad Relationship

As mentioned earlier, we originally met as graduate students. Crystal was a doctoral student and Chinyere was completing her Master of Education degree. This helped ease the transition into the professional dyad relationship. We saw ourselves as equal members of a partnership rather than participants in a hierarchical relationship between a university professor and classroom teacher. This proved to be important to the work as we often moved back and forth from the role of expert or leader and that of learner. These roles were fluid and interchangeable (Glover, Harris, Polson, & Boardman, 2017). For example, during Chinyere's first year as a teacher, she often came to Crystal for advice or suggestions about how to handle many of the obstacles she encountered. Crystal's years of experience as an early childhood classroom teacher and her role as a university professor gave her background from which to pull ideas and methods to support Chinyere and serve as a mentor. At the same time, Chinyere grew and took on leadership roles in which she helped inform Crystal about the nuances of her school environment, community, and colleagues. We moved seamlessly back and forth in our roles learning from and with each other as we encountered unforeseen obstacles in our work together, many of which are shared in this chapter.

Teachers Together

When Crystal visited the classroom during literacy instruction, she often worked with a small group of students, while Chinyere worked with a different group. This was important to our dyad relationship for a number of reasons. First, we wanted the children to recognize our partnership and see both of us as co-teachers in their literacy instruction. We also wanted to engage in roles that allowed each member of the dyad to design and implement curriculum that would best support the development of each child. By working with children in small groups, we were both able to observe and assess student performance in less restrictive settings. Ultimately, students came to view Crystal as another adult from whom they could learn and rely on for support.

Challenges in the Dyad Relationship

Although we experienced enormous success in our work together, our relationship as a dyad was not perfect. Given the busy nature of our own individual lives, we often failed to nurture our relationship when things became especially hectic. The timing of our project fell at one of the most intense times in both of our lives. We were both experiencing changes in our careers: Chinyere's status as a beginning teacher taking graduate classes along with Crystal's busy teaching schedule left little time to focus on our roles and relationships as members of a dyad. Initially, we made the mistake of focusing solely on our *work* as a dyad.

Our meeting times followed a tightly designed schedule which typically changed each semester based on our university schedules. We met promptly at our pre-arranged start time and immediately dove into our planned tasks for the day. There were times when our meetings became so intense that 15–20 minutes in, we would realize that we had barely said hello and hadn't even inquired about how the other was doing personally! For a while, it seemed as if things were "all business." Fortunately, those times did not persist; once we fell into a groove in our work lives, our personal relationship within the dyad relationship began to strengthen. During one of our first retreats as a cohort, we discovered that we shared many interests and similarities within our personal lives. We were both married with no children and loved to travel and experience different cultures. Those similarities shaped who we were as women of Color living in the south.

We also became aware of differences in our backgrounds, which influenced our roles as educational leaders. Our own educational experiences had a direct impact on the ways in which we viewed education and our expectations regarding the behaviors and academic performance of children of Color and emerging bi/multilingual children. For example, early in our partnership, we engaged in a conversation about African American Language (AAL), a distinct language widely spoken by African Americans in the United States (Boutte, 2007; Smitherman, 2006). As part of both her research and teaching, Crystal frequently shared classroom instructional strategies designed to both honor and support speakers of AAL. Crystal's interest in AAL was partly driven by her familiarity with the language and her own ability to code mesh (move back and forth and seamlessly blend between languages) and code switch (switch between two or more languages when appropriate) at will (Young, Barrett, & Lovejoy, 2014).

For Chinyere, AAL was intriguing, but for different reasons. Chinyere had concerns about the ways in which AAL is regarded within educational institutions. She recognized and understood that AAL is a legitimate language; however, she witnessed other teachers who felt that it was not legitimate. Chinyere wondered if other teachers thought that acknowledging AAL as a language system reflected poorly on African Americans and would lead to lower expectations for them. The more we read about AAL, the greater confidence we built in explaining the importance of validating AAL as part of students' linguistic repertoires and the art of translation—valuing students' cognitive, linguistic, and social abilities to use AAL, standardized English, and other languages according to the contexts in which they were most useful. On one occasion, Chinyere overheard a teacher admonishing a student for using AAL as "incorrect English." In response, Chinyere made sure that all of her students understood that they could speak whatever language felt most relevant to them in particular contexts. She helped them understand when to translate into standardized English as required by existing systems, testing for example. Looking back, we take this experience into our own further learning as we investigate the teaching of AAL histories, and connections to West African and Diaspora languages. This valuing of language was extended to all languages. Chinyere also informed teachers of the legalities of denying students the right to use their chosen languages in school, using the authority of position statements from the National Council of Teachers of English (2016) and the American Association for Applied Linguistics (1998).

It was through our ongoing discussions about language, and others like it, that we learned valuable lessons about working as a dyad. We learned that becoming a successful dyad doesn't require both members to share the same perspectives on all issues. Working as a dyad doesn't always involve consensus or conformity. Working as a dyad doesn't dissolve the unwavering stance that dyad members may hold about their work. However, working as a dyad *does* demand patience, respect for each other, commitment to ongoing study, persistence, and knowing that the work is a process. Joining with our community of learners within the PDCRT cohort helped strengthen and support our dyad relationship. Within this community, we used the guidelines below to negotiate our dyad relationship:

- Respect thoughts and ideas that differ from your own;
- Seek to understand and unpack diverse viewpoints;
- Recognize the potential for personal growth and development;
- Commit to the goal of honoring children.

These guidelines evolved as our work expanded over time to include topics that generated differences in opinion. We learned to communicate in ways, such as the Voxer app, that allowed both members of the dyad to be heard. As is the case in any relationship, we found that having the ability to demonstrate respect and humility when tensions occur helps maintain a strong, healthy, and lasting partnership.

Culturally Relevant and Sustaining Early Literacy Practices

This section will discuss the culturally relevant practices we implemented as part of our work. During our time together, we worked to *make evident the student expertise* that was a vital part of the classroom. We tapped into students' funds of knowledge (González, Moll, & Amanti, 2005) to uncover their expertise in a variety of areas. These practices demonstrated a strong reliance on *student autonomy and relationships* as integral to the implementation of our work. Students were given freedom and flexibility to approach their work in ways that highlighted their strengths and background knowledge. Further, we made consistent and deliberate strides to *supplement conventional assessments* with culturally relevant assessments when conventional assessments showed signs of bias and discrimination. Finally, we embraced *heritage as curriculum* when we aligned district literacy standards with culturally relevant assignments that focused on student heritage and cultural background. In this section, we detail each of our practices and provide vivid illustrations.

Making Student Expertise Visible

During the implementation of our project, we sought to recognize student expertise in different forms. By drawing on students' strengths and interests, we encouraged students to embrace their talents while working to strengthen areas in need of growth. In this way, we used our classroom "as a means of foregrounding the plural and dynamic nature of youths' identity" (Gutiérrez & Johnson, 2017, p. 247). Students were championed as leaders in our classroom and we readily turned over the reins once students had accomplished a skill. An example of this practice was the design and implementation of student-led lessons. One afternoon when Crystal entered the room during independent writing, she noticed a boy named Bralan (pseudonym) working intently on a presentation about Superheroes on his iPad. After having written a lesson plan on Superheroes (that was reviewed and given feedback from Chinyere), Bralan planned to present his lesson to the class the following day. He asked if he could practice it with Crystal and she readily agreed.

During his practice lesson, Bralan stopped patiently to answer Crystal's questions about the Superheroes who were the focus of this lesson. Bralan worked hard to ensure that Crystal was confident with the information in his lesson before administering the assessment he had designed to determine whether the students understood the lesson. This moment in which Bralan became the expert, teaching Crystal about Superheroes, was quite common in Chinyere's classroom. Students were given the authority to deepen their expertise and share it with others in ways that allowed us to "recognize the agentic, linguistic, sociocultural and sociopolitcal moves and practices that youth develop and leverage" (Gutiérrez & Johnson, 2017, p. 247). In the process, we were able to authentically assess students' literacy skills. For example, through Bralan's practice session and presentation, we learned that he was adept at constructing key details to support the main idea in his work. In this way, Chinyere's classroom became a space where children were able to "be vocal, be active, and reflective" (Garcia & Shirley, 2012, pp. 83–84) and demonstrate their expertise.

Student Autonomy and Relationships

One of Chinyere's greatest strengths as a classroom teacher is her ability to build relationships with students. She skillfully built strong, positive relationships with and between students. Chinyere wanted students to feel ownership of and autonomy in their learning. And while it all appears effortless, the classroom climate had been carefully crafted by Chinyere in her effort to embrace the children's backgrounds and interests.

For Chinyere, student autonomy became an outlet for culturally relevant practice. She allowed students the freedom to make choices about where and with whom they would work. Students were allowed the autonomy of deciding how they would like to demonstrate their knowledge. Students were also allowed to choose topics of interest when demonstrating their understanding of required literacy content such as organizing, summarizing, and synthesizing information. As such, we shared the belief that "making what youth do not know the primary focus of pedagogies is neither useful nor accurate in terms of assessing potential" (Gutiérrez & Johnson, 2017, p. 247).

An example of student choice and autonomy took place when students were required to demonstrate their understanding of animal adaptations and ecosystems. During a class study of animal adaptation, students were asked to create a super animal and describe the ecosystem the animal lives in, the roles undertaken by the animal, and any adaptations that their animal must make in order to survive easily in their environment. Students were asked to explain the creation of their animals. Figure 5.3 depicts a drawing of a student's super animal. In addition to the drawing, this student demonstrated knowledge of content-specific vocabulary, the understanding of animal adaptation, and ecosystems. The student also created succinct narratives explaining the creation and physical features of the created super animals. This task required that students to creatively demonstrate and apply their knowledge.

Supplementing Conventional Assessments

During our weekly meetings, we often discussed the district-mandated literacy assessments that children were required to take at the beginning, middle, and end of each year. These assessments were a frequent source of tension among teachers and even parents as the implementation of the assessments consumed a great deal of instructional time throughout the year, leaving classroom teachers little time to analyze the data the assessments supposedly revealed. In addition, district-mandated literacy assessments implemented consistently throughout the year frequently revealed inconsistent or partial comprehension results and failed to provide a true picture of all students' literacy abilities. Students who could clearly comprehend texts often scored below grade level. The assessments also left teachers with limited opportunities to digest the data in ways that could positively impact instruction and they had no support for acting on the inequities resulting from unjust assessment practices. In essence, the mandated assessments were deficit approaches which "view the languages, literacies, and cultural ways of being of many students and communities of color as deficiencies to be overcome if they

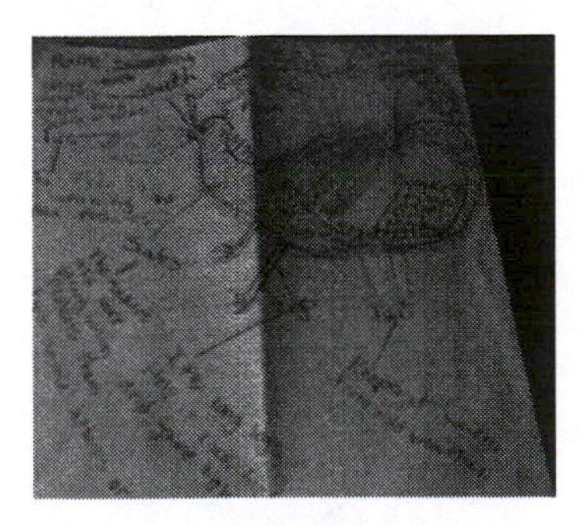

FIGURE 5.3 Student work sample—super animal.

are to learn the dominant language, literacy, and cultural ways of being demanded in schools" (Paris & Alim, 2014, p. 87). Finally, almost as soon as teachers completed the administration of one set of assessments and communicated the results to school administrators, it was nearly time to administer the assessments again.

The school-level assessments were equally problematic as they also offered little consideration for the perspectives and abilities of the children of Color and emerging bi/multilingual students who made up the majority of the school population. These homogenized assessments unfairly disadvantaged children who did not fit the White, middle-class ways of knowing and privileges for which they were designed (Clauser & Mazor, 1998; Freedle & Kostin, 1997; Qi & Marley, 2009; Saenz & Huer, 2003). They were conducted in English only, failing to account for the students' languages and cultural ways of knowing and being (Paris & Alim, 2014). Despite being a beginning teacher, it did not take long for Chinyere to recognize the biased nature of the assessments she was required to give. She immediately noticed "the existence of unexpected differences in test results for subgroups of similar ability levels within a tested population" (Kruse, 2016, p. 23) which were reflective not of students' failure but of failure of educational systems with Eurocentric, English-only norms. Although she was mandated to administer certain assessments, Chinyere did not allow the results of those assessments to paint an unfair picture of her students' abilities. Instead, she designed supplemental assessments such as teacher-made comprehension quizzes, oral retellings, and text-to-text connection webs to illustrate her students' knowledge of literacy content that might not otherwise manifest itself in a traditional English-only assessment. When we talked about the results of the school- and district-level literacy assessments, we pondered what might happen if district and state institutions recognized and acted on the need for children to be assessed in more culturally inclusive ways. We realized that without systemic change, the practices that we adopted would not be enough to sustain our students as they matriculated through their school careers.

We agreed that it was important to provide multiple ways for learners to demonstrate their knowledge and understanding authentically. For example, when district- and school-mandated testing required children to sit for long periods of time and answer questions on a paper-and-pencil test, we recognized that it was challenging for children who were adding English to their linguistic repertoires. As an alternative, we employed assessment that we hoped would allow them to draw on and show their own cultural strengths. For example, we allowed the children to work in small groups to summarize texts using dramatic reenactments, artifacts, and virtual retellings. In doing so, we created spaces for students to demonstrate knowledge using their own cultural competencies.

We found that our method of assessment appeared to be more engaging for students who demonstrated their enjoyment in working with and learning from their peers. When children completed assignments or assessments that in some way represented their own experiences and cultural background, they were more invested. For example, one small group of students enjoyed designing the dramatic reenactments and virtual retellings so much that they initiated similar activities on subsequent readings without being asked to do so. We witnessed moments like these over and over during the course of our work. Despite the success we experienced with these types of assessments, our inability to execute our work school- or district-wide further illustrates the need for institutional changes related to culturally biased assessments. For this reason, we continue to share the findings of our work as we work together with other educators and stakeholders to advocate for institutional change.

Families and Heritage as Curriculum

One of the literacy standards that children were required to master in second grade was to *investigate the children's abilities to generate, ask, and answer appropriate questions.* Learning now about culturally sustaining practice as that which seeks to "explore, honor, extend, and at times problematize heritage community practices" (Paris & Alim, 2014, p. 89), we see our work as beginning to address that characteristic. We chose to have the children design interview questions for their family members about their cultural, religious, and ethnic backgrounds. Students were encouraged to express their responses in ways that were meaningful to them and their cultural backgrounds. Next, we engaged the children creating culture quilts, or large, physical displays of their family interview responses. After interviewing their family members, each child represented the answers to their questions in a visual format or culture quilt (Figure 5.4). They included pictures and artifacts illustrating their family traditions. Since the families of the children in our class came from many different countries, with different ethnicities, and spoke several different languages, we sought to highlight these rich sources of community cultural wealth (Yosso, 2005). It was through this culturally relevant lens that 100% of students in the class were successful in meeting the requirements as outlined in the standard associated with this assignment: All of the children were able to successfully generate, ask, and answer appropriate questions about their family backgrounds. This form of assessment—accessing "multiple ways of speaking and being" (Paris & Alim, 2014, p. 89)—allowed us to see students' abilities whereas traditional assessments of the same standard had not.

Foregrounding Families

Families were regularly encouraged to share the funds of knowledge from their careers, hobbies, and talents outside of the classroom. Family members worked with their children to help others learn more about their backgrounds and cultural heritage. We knew that involving family members would help us activate the network of practices that are a part of people's everyday lives (Gonzalez et al., 2005; Gutierrez & Johnson, 2017, p. 252) and bring those practices alive in the classroom. A few of those practices are shared here.

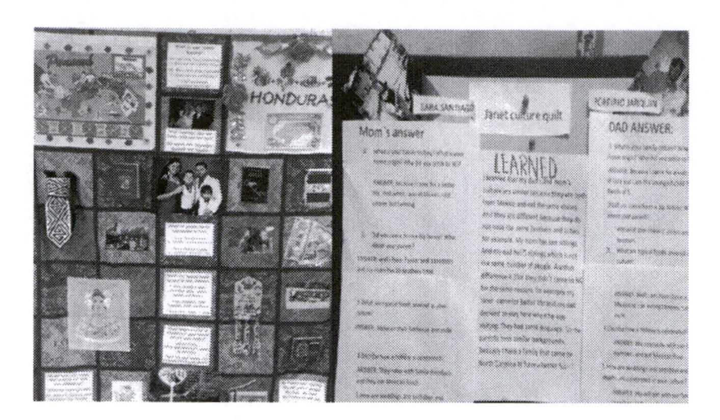

FIGURE 5.4 Student work samples—culture quilts.

Class Broadcast: The Cultural Enthusiast

When Chinyere's class sponsored a regular segment of the morning news on the school-wide closed-circuit television, family members of the children appeared on the show to share their knowledge and expertise about a variety of topics. During the class morning news segment students discussed and asserted who they were as cultural, social, and political beings. For example, during a special broadcast, students focused on the Ivory Coast. During this broadcast, one student who was an emerging bilingual interviewed his father about his journey to the United States. Joined by three of his classmates, the student engaged his father in a discussion about their history, currency, and his educational pursuits which led him to doctoral studies in statistics. During the weekly news broadcasts students interviewed parents, teachers, and other learners in the school to inquire about family stories, traditions, or rituals. The students invited special mystery guests to be on the broadcast. Guests represented a variety of countries such as Jamaica, Peru, France, and India. The interviews were conducted in the same style as StoryCorps interviews from the National Public Radio segment and children wrote their "news stories" for the morning news show as part of the classroom assignment. Parents joined students to make special appearances on the Cultural Enthusiast segment of the morning news. These appearances, coupled with classroom demonstrations and storytellings in which parents shared their lives, histories, and ways of being and doing, helped the children in the class recognize family members of their peers as extended members of their classroom community. As part of this culturally sustaining activity we hoped to "work toward reclamation of the histories, contributions, and possibilities of cultural communities" (Gutierrez & Johnson, 2017, p. 249) while challenging those "discourses that marginalize members of our communities" (Paris & Alim, 2014, p. 94).

Impromptu Home Visits

Shortly after starting her job as a new teacher, Chinyere discovered that many of her students lived in the same condominium complex as she did. Chinyere would frequently see the children and their parents while taking walks, at the supermarket, or at the university library. Hoping to capitalize on these informal meetings, Chinyere began to schedule impromptu visits with some of the mothers of students in her class who lived in her neighborhood. They met for coffee and discussed ways to strengthen family involvement, ways to enhance local and school events, and ways to ensure their child's academic success. For Chinyere, these meetings helped build a rapport and trust among parents with whom she might not otherwise encounter.

Engaging with students and their families in this way reinforced the importance of forming relationships with families to serve culturally relevant teaching. This enabled Chinyere to see the cultural currencies that parents and students brought with them to the classroom. Chinyere was able to appreciate and integrate those currencies into her curriculum and teaching. As a result, the parents felt valued as a part of the classroom community and Chinyere built stronger alliances with them.

Family Members in the Classroom

On many occasions family members would observe lessons or work their child or with a small reading group. Parents also led class instruction and attended class presentations (Figure 5.5). For example, Chinyere was fortunate to have regular parent volunteers. The parents would work with students during small groups during reader's workshop. Sometimes parents would lead discussions: on one occasion a parent was able to share his knowledge of Hebrew with the class.

FIGURE 5.5 Parent presentation: a parent joins her daughters to present relevant information on their home country of El Salvador.

Students eagerly listened to his explanation of how Hebrew is written and read. When family members had a question or concern, they willingly communicated by email, phone, or text messaging. We listened to families' voices and incorporated their experiences and perspectives into instruction. For example, on one occasion we assigned a reading about *Día de los Muertos*/The Day of the Dead. Students who celebrated this holiday remembering family and friends who have died were excited to read about and share this aspect of their culture with their classmates. Having family interest and engagement in what was taking place in the classroom inspired not only what would be taught, but how we would extend the curriculum to the wider school and community. As a result of having an open-door policy and Chinyere taking the initiative to go to families in their communities, we were able to engage parents as mutual learning partners focused on providing what is best for their child academically, socially, and emotionally. We were able to collaborate with parents on instructional goals and how to best motivate their children to successfully engage in learning.

Challenges in Our Work

Although we felt that our work was fruitful, we faced our share of challenges. For one, we had to contend with outside influences which made it difficult not to succumb to attempts to stifle and detract from our efforts. There were naysayers within the academic setting who held little regard for culturally relevant practice. However, we were able to persevere in our work despite the attempts to prevent our progress. For example, when other teachers resisted our attempts to depart from culturally biased assessment tools by insisting that we exclusively use the district-mandated assessment, we were able to persist and introduce more culturally inclusive measures of assessing student performance.

Another challenge we faced pertained to schedule changes within the school. We designed our literacy block to provide small group, whole group, and individualized instruction grounded in culturally relevant practice. To accomplish this, we carefully outlined a schedule that would allow us to implement each of these important components at specific times. Frequent changes in the school schedule forced us to abandon our initial plans and to implement a more flexible schedule. At first, we struggled to find time to implement all of the components we planned for the literacy block. We were encumbered by the grade-level schedule that was set to accommodate ability-based reading groups. As time passed, we were able to modify our initial plans to allow for both the grade-level schedule and our own class plan based on culturally relevant practice.

Other bureaucratic measures temporarily disrupted our work from time to time. Students were required to participate in district-mandated testing for weeks at a time. During those times, we were unable to implement our work as planned. Student anxiety and stress from those assessments forced us to stop and reassure students before re-engaging in our work following the tense testing periods. Overall, the challenges served as minor setbacks, and in some cases, learning opportunities. We faced each obstacle as a surmountable task and resolved to maintain our progress forward.

Conclusion: Extending the Village

As educators committed to equity in education, we readily embraced the initial call of the PDCRT to champion culturally relevant early literacy instruction. At the outset of the project, our work was guided by the efforts of pioneers in the fields of culturally relevant pedagogy and multicultural literacy instruction in the early childhood education. Together, we read the works of Ladson-Billings (1995), Genishi and Dyson (2009), Delpit (2012), Long, Volk, Baines, and Tisdale (2013), and Souto-Manning (2013). As our work progressed and we recognized the importance of "sustain[ing] linguistic, literate, and cultural pluralism as part of schooling for positive transformation" (Alim & Paris, 2017, p. 1), we began to explore the work of Paris and Alim (2014, 2017), Kinloch (2017), and McCarty and Lee (2014). In our ongoing quest to become consumers and leaders in teaching that challenges the dominant White Gaze in pedagogy and practice, we sought and continue to seek to enrich and expand our work so that it consistently overturns pedagogies that privilege and oppress.

In this chapter, we described a handful of practices implemented in Chinyere's classroom (Table 5.1). We also highlighted ways in which we capitalized on our dyad partnership to challenge our thinking. We designed instructional strategies based on our desire to honor the cultural practices, beliefs, and values of the students with whom we worked and to expand the cultural repertoires of every student.

Can this work be sustained? We believe that it must but that to do so, the examples of teaching like Chinyere's and its positive outcomes need to be utilized in discussions of policy as illustrative, but not formulaic representations, of what is possible for every student given institutional commitment to change. As warriors in this fight, we urge early childhood literacy educators to move forward in the quest to enact culturally relevant teaching and to turn it into sustaining pedagogies that have the potential to change the future of our worlds. In that quest, we embrace the truth we have found in San Pedro's (2017) belief that:

> When relationships rooted in culturally situated respect, reciprocity, and responsibility are created, fostered and nurtured, they lead to classroom discussion rooted not in academic debate, where conversations are won or lost; rather it leads to the co-creation of sacred truth spaced rooted in humanizing dialogue; where meaning is made in the spaces between our stories because of—and not in spite of—our differences. (p. 103)

TABLE 5.1 Culturally relevant and sustaining classroom practices.

	CRT Practice	*Description*
Making Evident Student Expertise	Student-Created Lesson Plans	• Children select a topic of interest to teach to the other children in the class. • Once their topic has been approved by the teacher, students conduct research on the topic and design a lesson plan to teach the other children in the class. • As part of the lesson plan, children practice writing assessment questions and apply their knowledge of sequencing, cause and effect, and fact vs fiction. • Students develop oral language skills as they present their lessons and hold class discussions on the topic.
Student Autonomy and Relationships	Cultural Music	• Music from a variety of genres reflecting the culture, ethnicity, and interests of the children in the classroom is played throughout the day. • The music serves as a backdrop and sets the tone for an inviting classroom climate. The music selected is based on student and family preferences.
	Seating Choice	• Children are given options to complete their individual and small group assignments at various locations throughout the classroom. • Children may choose to sit at desks, tables, on rugs, bean bags, or large floor pillows. • Children use clipboards to brace their writing and have access to individual whiteboards to complete their work.
Supplementing Conventional Assessments	Alternative Assessments	• Teachers provide alternatives to traditional assessment measures for children in the classroom. • These assessments are used in conjunction with traditional assessment tools to measure student performance. • Examples include: portfolios, photographs, video recordings, interviews, and student presentations.
Heritage as Curriculum	Culture Quilts	• Students generate a list of 10 questions to ask members of their family about their family background. • Students interview parents and record their responses to the questions. • Students create a presentation of their findings as well as an artifact representing their family.
	Cultural Enthusiast	• Students retell family traditions, stories, or rituals as part of a class writing assignment. • Students appear alongside parents on school-wide morning news show to share their stories with members of the school community.

References

Alim, H. S., & Paris, D. (2017). What is culturally sustaining pedagogy and why does it matter? In D. Paris & H. S. Alim (Eds.), *Culturally sustaining pedagogies: Teaching and learning for justice in a changing world* (pp. 1–24). New York, NY: Teachers College Press.

American Association for Applied Linguistics. (1998). *Researchers and educators advocate wider understanding of language diversity*. Retrieved from https://www.aaal.org/position-statements##

Boutte, G. S. (2007). Teaching African American English speakers: Expanding educators and student repertoires. In M. Brisk (Ed.), *Language, culture, and community in teacher education* (pp. 47–70). New York, NY: Routledge.

Charmaz, K. (2014). *Constructing grounded theory*. Thousand Oaks, CA: Sage.

Clauser, B. E., & Mazor, K. M. (1998). Using statistical procedures to identify differentially functioning test items. *Educational Measurement: Issues and Practice*, 17, 31–44. doi:10.1111/j.1745-3992.1998.tb00619.x

Delpit, L. (2012). *"Multiplication is for White people": Raising expectations for other people's children*. New York, NY: The New Press.

Dominguez, M. (2017). "Se Hace Puentes al Andar": Decolonial teacher education as a needed bridge to culturally sustaining and revitalizing pedagogies. In D. Paris & H. S. Alim (Eds.), *Culturally sustaining pedagogies: Teaching and learning for justice in a changing world* (pp. 225–245). New York, NY: Teachers College Press.

Freedle, R., & Kostin, I. (1997). Predicting Black and White differential item functioning in verbal analogy performance. *Intelligence*, 24(3), 417–444.

Garcia, J., & Shirley, V. (2012). Performing decolonization: Lessons learned from Indigenous youth, teachers and leaders' engagement with critical indigenous pedagogy. *Journal of Curriculum Theorizing*, 28(2), 76–91.

Genishi, C., & Dyson, A. H. (2009). *Children, language, and literacy: Diverse learners in diverse times*. New York, NY: Teachers College Press.

Glover, C., Harris, C., Polson, B., & Boardman, A. (2017). Creating supportive and subversive spaces as professional dyads enacting culturally relevant teaching. *Early Years*, 37, 47–61.

González, N., Moll, L. & Amanti, C. (Eds.). (2005). *Fund of knowledge: Theorizing practices in households and classrooms*. Mahwah, NJ: Erlbaum.

Gutiérrez, K. D., & Johnson, P. (2017). Understanding identity sampling and cultural repertoires: Advancing learning in justice pedagogies. InD. Paris & H. S. Alim (Eds.), *Culturally sustaining pedagogies: Teaching and learning for justice in a changing world* (pp. 247–260). New York, NY: Teachers College Press.

Kinloch, V. (2017). "You ain't making me write." In D. Paris & H. S. Alim (Eds.), *Culturally sustaining pedagogies: Teaching and learning for justice in a changing world* (pp. 25–43). New York, NY: Teachers College Press.

Kruse, A. J. (2016). Cultural bias in testing: A review of literature and implications in music education. *Update: Applications of Research in Music Education*, 35, 23–31.

Ladson-Billings, G. (1995). But that's just good teaching! The case for culturally relevant pedagogy. *Theory into Practice*, 34(3), 159–165.

Long, S., Volk, D., Baines, J., & Tisdale, C. (2013). "We've been doing it your way long enough": Syncretism as a critical process. *Journal of Early Childhood Literacy*, 13, 418–439.

Lorde, A. (1986). *Our dead behind us: Poems*. New York, NY: WW Norton & Company.

McCarty, T., & Lee, T. (2014). Critical culturally sustaining/revitalizing pedagogy and Indigenous education sovereignty. *Harvard Educational Review*, 84, 101–124.

Mohanty, J. (2000). *The self and its other: Philosophical essays*. Oxford: Oxford University Press.

Morrison, T. (1998, March). *From an interview on Charlie Rose*. Public Broadcasting Service. Retrieved from http://www.youtube.com/watch?v=F4vIGvKpT1c

National Council of Teachers of English. (2016). *Conference on college composition and communication statement on ebonics*. Retrieved from http://www2.ncte.org/statement/ebonics/

Paris, D., & Alim, H. S. (2014). What are we seeking to sustain through culturally sustaining pedagogy? A loving critique forward. *Harvard Educational Review*, 84, 85–100.

Paris, D., & Alim, H. S. (2017). *Culturally sustaining pedagogies: Teaching and learning for justice in a changing world*. New York, NY: Teachers College Press.

Qi, C. H., & Marley, S. C. (2009). Differential item functioning analysis of the Preschool Language Scale-4 between English-speaking Hispanic and European American children from low-income families. *Topics in Early Childhood Special Education*, 29, 171–180. doi:10.1177/0271121409332674

San Pedro, T. J. (2017). This stuff interests me: Re-centering indigenous paradigms in colonizing schooling spaces. In D. Paris & S. Alim (Eds.), *Culturally sustaining pedagogy: Teaching and learning for justice in a changing world*. New York, NY: Teachers College Press.

Saenz, T. I., & Huer, M. B. (2003). Testing strategies involving least biased language assessment of bilingual children. *Communication Disorders Quarterly*, 24, 184–193. doi:10.1177/152574010302400404 01

Smitherman, G. (2006). *Words from the mother: Language and African Americans*. New York, NY: Routledge.

Souto-Manning, M. (2013). *Multicultural teaching in the early childhood classroom: Approaches, strategies, and tools, preschool–2nd grade*. New York, NY: Teachers College Press.

Yosso, T. J. (2005). Whose culture has capital? A critical race theory discussion of community cultural wealth. *Race, Ethnicity and education*, 8, 69–91.

Young, V. A., Barrett, R., & Lovejoy, K. B. (2014). *Other people's English: Code-meshing, code-switching, and African American literacy*. New York, NY: Teachers College Press.

6

CULTURALLY RELEVANT PEDAGOGIES AS THE NORM

Lessons Learned, Action Steps, and Questions to Help Us Move Toward Culturally Sustaining Pedagogies

Dinah Volk and Erin T. Miller

If not me, then who?

We begin this final chapter with words from Carmen Tisdale, teacher and member of PDCRT's original advisory board. Her words capture the sense of responsibility shared by all involved in this book to help create the change necessary to ensure that those who inform educational programs, policies, and practices commit to "value cultural and linguistic sharing across difference, to sustain and support bi- and multilingualism and bi- and multiculturalism" (Paris, 2012, p. 95). The normalization of such culturally relevant teaching as the foundation of teaching for all students has been called for repeatedly (Baines, Tisdale, & Long, 2018; Ladson-Billings, 2012) and its importance in *sustaining* our rich multicultural, multilingual societies has been emphasized in the work of Paris (2012) and Paris and Alim (2014, 2017b) as described in Chapter One. Building from culturally relevant pedagogies, Paris and Alim describe culturally sustaining pedagogies (CSP) as those which "perpetuate and foster— … sustain—linguistic literate, and cultural pluralism as a part of the democratic project of schooling" (2014, p. 95). From this transformational perspective, "CSP exists wherever education sustains the lifeways of communities who have been and continue to be damaged and erased through schooling" (Paris, 2019).

The teachers and teacher educators in this book and the PDCRT project itself embrace this stance and its resistance to "policies and practices that have the explicit goal of creating a monocultural and monolingual society" (Paris, 2012, p. 95). The frustrations as well as the successes generated by our work remind us that sustaining a democratic project of schooling that normalizes multilingualism and multiculturalism and rejects the dominant White Gaze (Morrison, 1998) requires the transformation not only of day-to-day work in classrooms but also of the policies, practices, dispositions, and traditions that govern the institutions of schooling.

Thus, this book is about culturally relevant teaching but it also reflects the authors' interest in understanding and moving toward culturally sustaining work. As do the editors and the chapter authors, we use the term *culturally sustaining pedagogy* with respect and caution, not wanting to claim it as a descriptor of our work since the project was originally anchored in Ladson-Billings' (1995) conceptualization of *culturally relevant pedagogy*. We acknowledge that the work described here moves *in the direction of* sustaining cultural and linguistic pluralism in schools and society but that it is only a beginning. As Ladson-Billings (2014, 2017) wrote about the corruptions of culturally relevant teaching by those who take a tourist approach to cultural competence, a test-based approach to student achievement, and surface-level approaches to building a critical consciousness, we are also leery of taking on the term *culturally sustaining pedagogy* without further study, reflection, and experience. Thus, in this chapter, we share lessons learned in the work of four dyads as they embraced culturally relevant teaching and move *toward* culturally sustaining teaching and we raise questions for self-reflection that we believe can propel the movement to sustain.

As described in Chapter One, the educators whose stories are shared here worked together for two years in diverse, multilingual classrooms across the United States in the Professional Dyads and Culturally Relevant Teaching (PDCRT) project. The project aims to validate social, cultural, linguistic, and heritage knowledge of the children, families, and communities most often sidelined, ignored, or misrepresented/distorted in typical curricula and to curricularize or "make into curriculum" (Paris & Alim, 2017a, n.p.) and normalize those diversities in classroom practice. That is, the PDCRT project is concerned with countering pedagogies, practice, and policy dominated by Eurocratic ideologies. Also as noted in Chapter One, we use the term *Eurocratic* (King & Swartz, 2014) instead of *Eurocentric*, to acknowledge the "officially sanctioned constraints … on knowledge, through systems [like education] that maintain Euro-American authority and hegemony" (p. 13). Eurocratic implies a hegemonic system that establishes single truths grounded in Euro-American accomplishments, histories, cultures, and narratives. Our work seeks to dismantle and replace this ideology and the practice derived from it, "divesting from whiteness and the ways whiteness castes white normed practices and bodies as superior" (Paris, 2019). This is not to reject European contributions to the world's knowledge, but to insist that what has been normalized in curriculum must be broadened as well as interrogated and challenged for its Eurocratic nature, which includes inaccuracies, omissions, distortions, and mistellings (Baines et al., 2018).

In this chapter, as two of the founders of PDCRT, we begin by sharing the stance and goals that guided the project from its inception, drawing on retrospective interviews we conducted with the project's first board members, some teachers, some teacher educators, some of them also dyad members (Susi Long, Erin Miller, Dinah Volk, Mariana Souto-Manning, Eileen Blanco-Dougherty, Carmen Tisdale, Julia López-Robertson, and Bilal Polson). Next, we celebrate the work of the dyads as described in Chapters Two through Five as well as noting their challenges, reflecting on lessons learned, and advocating for perspectives and action steps to be taken. Finally, we provide a discussion of the PDCRT practices illuminated in this book as initial elements in a move toward Paris and Alim's (2017b) conceptualization of *culturally sustaining pedagogies*. We ask if and how this work reflects teaching that rejects the White Gaze as dominant, and instead liberates teaching from that gaze to create pedagogies in which multilingualism and multiculturalism are embraced as the norm. We also raise questions about the sustainability of this work and the self-reflection and risk-taking required to guide educators toward better understanding how to better create culturally sustaining educational institutions.

Context for Lessons Learned: PDCRT Stance and Goals

Like other members of the leadership team of the first PDCRT cohort, we were initially drawn to the development of this project because we knew that the insights of children and families as well as educators of Color were rarely heard in the mainstream literature in literacy and early childhood education. At multiple levels, their expertise continued to be marginalized, silenced, and dismissed. As teacher educators seeking textbooks for our courses, we found a dearth of relevant sources in which teachers and teacher educators of Color shared their perspectives and practices. The teachers on the leadership team, like preservice teachers in our courses, had asked over and over again, "But, what does this *look* like? How would I *do* this?" when discussing equity-based practices. As a consequence, we were all drawn to the development of a long-term project that (a) expanded the existing literature by theorizing culturally relevant pedagogies and provided practical examples from early childhood (K–3) classrooms and (b) was characterized by the leadership of educators of Color.

Also at the core of PDCRT and just as important, is the development of mutual mentorships between teachers and teacher educators. Too many projects, we felt, were rooted in university–school hierarchies where university faculty are viewed or act as more knowledgeable than classroom teachers when, in actuality, every teacher educator's work is informed by the work of teachers, children, and families. In sum, our aim was to disrupt and replace discriminatory content, practices, and hierarchies at multiple levels in our field.

The initial goals of PDCRT provide one aspect of the context for the practices implemented by the dyads highlighted in this book. They set the stage for the work and provide a way to understand and evaluate it. Thus, the lessons learned by these dyads are directly related to the goals described in this section, as remembered and interpreted by the first PDCRT board members. Through our interviews with them, two goals emerged as overarching aspects of the structure of the project: (a) developing, implementing, and documenting culturally relevant pedagogies and (b) creating mutual mentorships within the teacher–teacher educator partnerships. Notably these overlapped with other goals that were highlighted at different times during the implementation of the dyads' work. Clarity about goals as well as the flexibility to refine and rethink them were necessary; foundational aspects were constantly being revised and enhanced. That said, the project aimed to accomplish the goals listed in Figure 6.1 that appear as subheadings and are discussed in the following sections.

Develop Culturally Relevant Pedagogies in Early Childhood (PreK–Grade 3) Classrooms

Centering historically marginalized students and their languages and culture in order to foster insights about their brilliance and construct a culturally relevant curriculum was a central goal. A key aspect of that goal was fostering the children's academic success, and finding "ways to showcase student performance and student success based in this work."[1] And it was important that we were "doing that work unapologetically." One participant recalled that Susi Long and Carmen Tisdale's collaboration in Carmen's and later Janice Baines' classroom to develop and examine culturally relevant practices provided a model for how the work could look, and remembers "their model was built out of both of their uncompromising beliefs in children, particularly in Children of Color who have been historically marginalized." Another participant shared her feeling that the project was grounded in a commitment to the belief "that families … can be participants in curriculum construction in ways often unexplored and just emerging."

The project's contribution to understanding culturally relevant practices in early childhood classrooms specifically cannot be overstated. As a participant explained, "the voice of early childhood was not at the table," alluding to the concentration of work on culturally relevant teaching at the secondary level. This focus was critical because, as she remembered, "[early childhood] always seems to be like the stepchild of the school." Another agreed that a project goal was to provide "solid examples [of culturally relevant teaching] for new [early childhood] teachers." Teacher educators in the dyads also wanted examples to share with their students who could often articulate the theory but had little idea what it meant in practice.

1. Develop culturally relevant pedagogies in early childhood (PreK–Grade 3) classrooms
2. Create mutual mentorships and dismantle university–school hierarchies
3. Provide a support system for getting started with culturally relevant teaching
4. Prioritize diverse classrooms and teachers of Color, cultivating their professional leadership
5. Transform early childhood spaces into places for critical conversations

FIGURE 6.1 PDCRT Goals

Create Mutual Mentorships and Dismantle University–School Hierarchies

Over and over, participants affirmed the importance of the project's goal to develop mutual mentorships and dismantle top-down, university–school hierarchies. The resulting mentorships were described in a variety of ways, but all participants interviewed remembered attention to the "balance of power." As one board and dyad member explained, "it was a mutual learning process." Another board member reflected, the "university folks were not bringing a model to the teachers to implement but they were to implement jointly planned work."

The goal of mutual mentorships, though, was harder to actualize than it was to conceptualize initially. Hierarchical structures were often so ingrained that it was sometimes difficult to imagine more congruent relationships and put them into practice. This was obvious in a range of ways described later in this chapter. These experiences led us to affirm that the creation of mutual mentorships was necessary for the project's success. According to a board member, "Our experiences working in schools as university faculty convinced us that top down imposition of 'new' curricula was not viable and that CRT [culturally relevant teaching] might *only* be generated out of more equal collaborations."

Provide a Support System for Getting Started with Culturally Relevant Teaching

Another goal described by cohort leaders was to help teachers simply get started in generating and trying out new practices. This is often an unrecognized challenge in pedagogical innovation. Over the years, we have heard teachers with whom we worked say they had great ideas, but they just did not know where to start. A board member and teacher said she always wanted to explore culturally relevant practices but would get "stumped at the beginning." Given the dyad structure, a cohort support system, and project guidelines that asked dyads to start with their concerns and questions, develop a system for discussing professional readings with classroom possibilities in mind, and develop a data collection process, the teachers and teacher educators were able to start and work from there.

Providing mutual support across dyads, including sharing insight and advice, suggesting direction, and cheerleading, was a related goal. As teacher–teacher educator partners worked together to overcome challenges, they also relied on other dyads. This proved especially important for teachers who had a hard time finding a support system in their schools.

Prioritize Diverse Classrooms and Teachers of Color, Cultivate Leadership

Much research and practical writing about early literacy practices has taken place in classrooms filled with White, middle-class, monolingual children taught by White teachers. Intentionally committed to countering this, the PDCRT project was designed to take place in classrooms that reflected the racial, linguistic, socioeconomic diversity of students who are often marginalized, ignored, misunderstood, and oppressed in academic spaces. The PDCRT mission also put a "strong priority on teachers of Color" described as "grossly underrepresented in the profession while at the same time there was a growing percentage of children of Color in schools," notably without "adequate supports." A board member/dyad member noted that by "investing" in teachers of Color "we would be investing in our development as well." The project aim was to bring these voices to the fore and be guided by them.

Thus, the commitment to cultivating leadership among educators of Color was another critical goal for PDCRT that was also relevant to the National Council of Teachers of English (NCTE), our funding organization. At the time PDCRT was conceived, the leadership of NCTE was not richly diverse. As a consequence of our work, as delineated later in this chapter, PDCRT members are now leaders at many levels of the organization in addition to engaging in leadership roles on local and national levels.

Transform Early Childhood Spaces into Places for Critical Conversations

A key corruption of culturally relevant teaching noted by Ladson-Billings (2014) is lack of attention or active resistance to developing children's critical consciousness as well as teaching children strategies to act on their critiques. In order to tackle and ameliorate this corruption, a major PDCRT goal articulated by participants was the creation of early childhood classrooms as places where critical work happens, where dominant structures that maintain inequity can be analyzed and action strategies can be explored. One teacher argued that young children could have "these [difficult] conversations … even though they're small." Another agreed that young children are perfectly capable of naming "what's fair and unfair" in the world. Still another explained that participants were united in their belief that "young children can grapple with and pursue their own questions about complex issues of race, justice, discrimination, immigration, etc. with the skillful scaffolding of teachers, and come to deeper understandings." Examples throughout the preceding chapters provide evidence of these convictions.

Lessons Learned and Action Steps: Reflections/Advocacy for Culturally Relevant Teaching

In this section, we advocate for perspectives and practices grounded in lessons learned from the work of the four PDCRT dyads described in Chapters Two through Five, highlighting their insights and practices within the context established by the insights of the original advisory board members. We discuss aspects of the work that were effective and those that were not, as well as challenges met and not met. We begin each section below with an overview of participants' experiences, weaving together the specifics that the dyads described in the preceding chapters, and conclude with recommended perspectives and action steps. These lessons and action steps may be useful to educators seeking to implement culturally relevant pedagogies, create mutual mentorships between schools and universities, and move in the direction of culturally sustaining work.

Lesson #1: Nurture Distinct Practices in Each Classroom Context; There is No Formula

Experiences

In each PDCRT locale, classroom work grew out of the interests, concerns, lives, and questions of the children and their families. Lessons learned about the need for distinct—not cookie-cutter—practices came from the determination of the dyads to listen to, forefront, and curricularize what they learned about students, families, and communities in combination with their own interests and expertise. Because each classroom was embedded in a specific social/cultural/historical context and because of distinctions among the teachers, children, and families, the teaching and learning in each classroom were distinct. There was no formula. For example, preschool activities in Patricia's classroom differed from those in Chinyere's and Alicia's second grades, which were different from each other. In the same way, projects undertaken by Alicia and Bilal during an election period were different than those a year later, while Julia and Mary Jade's mothers' group responded to a principal's specific request after an immigration raid; and projects in Bilal and Alicia's school on suburban Long Island with a large immigrant Latinx population differed from those in urban neighborhoods with different demographics such as Chinyere's.

Still, when each dyad presented their work at day-long meetings at the NCTE conferences and at our three-day Summer Institutes, the richness of each dyad's work provided insights for every other dyad. In other words, we all learned from ways that each dyad appropriated the tenets of culturally relevant teaching for *their* students at *a particular* moment in time. We watched in awe as each dyad pinpointed their own questions and concerns and figured out what culturally relevant teaching and learning meant in their classroom and community and then proceeded to implement it.

Perspectives and Action Steps

Culturally relevant pedagogies are not marginal but they are "the work" to be accomplished "unapologetically." In order to do this and provide fertile ground for teachers to be responsive to their children and families in distinct not formulaic ways, a central structure can be useful to provide support, promote teachers' responsibility in the move toward change, and facilitate opportunities for the group to study and talk together. For us, the central structure of a board, guidelines, required data collection, and regular meetings, readings, and group presentations pushed everyone's knowledge and understanding to higher levels. In this decentralized format, which offers no set of activities to replicate but many examples to inform and motivate, many teachers will flourish. Educators can all learn from each other and be inspired by the creativity and tenacity of others.

Lesson #2: Address Power Differentials

Experiences

Challenging and replacing the power differentials inherent in our roles and positionalities (classroom teacher and university teacher educator; teacher and family member; educators of Color and White educators; White teacher educators and pre-service teachers of Color) was hard and central to the work of PDCRT. Whether these relationships were oppressive or productive, they were the relationships that were common and that PDCRT sought to address. While everyone professed to agree that dismantling university–school hierarchies was important, teacher educators sometimes found it hard to identify when their practices oppressed dyad partners and, once aware, it was hard to craft new practices. For example, teacher educators sometimes thought they were advocating for their dyad partners by answering emails directed to both or speaking for them in meetings and presentations. At the same time, classroom teachers sometimes acquiesced to their teacher educator partners because of the same learned hierarchies, feeling less intellectual, less educated, and consequently, less confident. As dyad member, Bilal reflected on these experiences as an undergraduate and graduate student: "For me … even though my relationships with university professors were always good … it was always they were the mentors and I was always the mentee, right? That was what it was. It was never questioned."

We knew that, in order to co-construct new relationships based on mutual mentorship within university and school systems set up to reinforce top-down ideologies, teacher educators in dyads would have to give up power so that teachers could take up power. This involved trust, intense conversations, commitment to and reminders of the project goals of mutual mentorship, and a critical analysis of power and privilege in society. These practices and qualities were evident in all the dyad work described in previous chapters in which the development of mutual mentorships was a common theme. Patricia and Kindel honored each other's skills and worked to communicate their more equal relationship to the children. Mary Jade and Julia wrote, "As a dyad we share that sense of trust and responsibility with each other," and went on to describe how it carried over into their work with families. Chinyere and Crystal also worked as co-teachers and continually explored their differing backgrounds and perspectives to further their learning from each other.

Discussions about racial power differentials were also key, given the pervasive White Gaze (Morrison, 1998) that tends to dominate educational spaces and is rarely interrogated by White educators. While the project was committed to participants who were educators of Color, the project has also included several White participants, some of whom noticed their own tendency to "have the answers" and value more Eurocentric ways of leading, organizing, and collaborating. One White board member commented on how easily she fell into a dominating stance by, for example, having "the" answers and offering an excessive number of ideas, even while in the minority, as is typical of those perpetuating White supremacy: "[W]e also need to pay attention to how easily we [as White people] can dominate as that colonizers' mentality rears its ugly head when we least expect it." In retrospect, members of the leadership team wondered what more could have been done about these challenges as we struggled to disrupt and change the institutional status quo.

Power dynamics occurred within dyads as well, sometimes related to gender, sometimes intersecting with job status and race/ethnicity. For example, Alicia, a Latina dual language teacher, and Bilal, self-identified as African American and African Latino (then the assistant principal of the school where Alicia taught and her supervisor), sometimes struggled to engage with each other as mutual learners. Alicia is the wife of a White police officer and they are parents of biracial children who they identify as Afro/Latino and Indigenous/White/Latino; Bilal and his wife are the parents of Afro/Latino boys. During the onset of the #BlackLivesMatter movement, Alicia and Bilal committed to deep conversations about the role of White policemen and the realities of Black males that were difficult at times. But as they describe in their chapter, they learned from each other as they committed to sometimes "walk away from the conversation but not from each other," always coming back to the talk necessary to understand each other's point of view.

Perspectives and Action Steps

As a result of PDCRT experiences, we find that mutual commitment to project goals is necessary to disrupt the traditional, socially embedded differentials of power and privilege as is commitment to honest talk in which all question their beliefs and practices. In particular, our dyad experiences in this and other organizations and projects pointed out how critical it is that White educators listen to *and hear* the voices of educators of Color no matter the setting. Collaborative discussions of readings that provide an analysis of social structures, racism, and programs that challenge them can create a context for learning. Making power differentials explicit can help everyone change their practice as can providing models such as Alicia and Bilal's.

It can be helpful to have a specific project vision and goals about mutual mentorship that participants can turn to when dyad relationships become troubled. For us, goal-related aspects that were particularly helpful were being explicit about racial representation in leadership roles, the dyads' ownership of their own data, and the project ethos promoting the collaborative sharing and disseminating of data. When challenges arise in relation to these and other issues and cannot be resolved by participants, it is important to have project leaders who can uphold the project goals and provide mediation through honest discussion and sharing of feelings and purpose, grounded in research that can bring insight to issues of racial, gender, and positional bias.

Lesson #3: Recognize that Relationships Are Fundamental and They Take Time to Build

Experiences

Relationships within dyads, across the project, and with families were at the heart of our work and were essential to it. As a participant noted,

> A lot of my belief systems that I thought were peripheral to the work I learned *was* the work. So, for example the grace, the humility, the self-reflective piece, the collaboration, the co-mentorship, the honoring, the spiritual aspects, the reverence.

We were challenged, especially as we worked to nurture relationships across racial, linguistic, and class lines and among participants at different levels of the education hierarchy.

The creation of the dyad relationships stands out as a theme in all preceding chapters and is crystalized in the Valdéz poem cited by Julia and Mary Jade that references the Mayan principle, "You are my other me." As discussed above, the dyads explored and sometimes struggled with creating such relationships. Through this process they all came to realize that mentoring each other took a great deal of attention and time. In particular, it took time for trust to develop in order for the dyads to be able to collaborate and venture into necessary, difficult conversations. In the project as a whole, there was never enough time, particularly given all that each dyad wanted to accomplish as well as the pressure from traditional power sources for measurable results that, as one dyad member put it, always seemed to be "due yesterday." Sometimes the dyad relationship suffered in the process.

Dyad members' relationships with other teachers in their schools were somewhat different in each setting. Chinyere's colleagues joined her study group and book club and participated in the school-wide professional development session that she and Crystal led. Some of Bilal and Alicia's teacher colleagues were cautious at first but eager, for example, to organize a museum in their classes after they saw how effective it was in Alicia's. In Julia and Mary Jade's case, other teachers felt (not surprisingly) overwhelmed when faced with a new project, this one about culturally relevant teaching, so Julia and Mary Jade "took a breather" and, instead and at the principal's request, developed the Latinx mothers' group.

All four dyads writing in this book had the advantage of being able to build on the welcoming relationships established with families by the schools in which they worked. As noted, all four teachers constructed curriculum that leveraged the languages and cultures of their families and communities as well as making them a part of learning activities through interviews and discussions, the collection of family stories and rituals, and as audience members for presentations. Family members were viewed as experts in these contexts. Moving beyond these curricular innovations, the PDCRT dyads also shared information with parents about topics such as translanguaging and responded to parents' concerns about their children's schooling, providing them with tools for engaging with school personnel and advocating for their children. Julia and Mary Jade's Latinx mothers' group was not a "how-to" but began by positioning the mothers as active members who could contribute to the school community. Learning as well as respect were reciprocal between this dyad and the mothers. As Mary Jade and Julia wrote in their chapter, "For us this meant giving time for the relationship with families to grow, having the patience that things were not going to happen immediately and understanding that we were not in control..."

Perspectives and Action Steps

Building relationships with colleagues, children, and families while co-constructing culturally relevant pedagogies takes time and energy. This means a commitment to creating spaces within the project for building relationships is critical. Sometimes necessary paperwork relevant to the project and other pre-set project goals must become secondary to devoting time for conversations among participants in which everyone questions their beliefs and listens to each other. Such conversations can be nurtured through joint readings, sharing of strategies, highlighting models, and developing the habit of critique in supportive settings. Relationships with colleagues beyond the project who can provide support and become collaborators also have to be carefully nurtured. As Alicia and Chinyere discovered, providing information, demonstrating the powerful outcomes of culturally relevant teaching, and being patient and flexible through colleagues' concerns and, sometimes, rejection can be fruitful. Trusting relationships with parents can be nurtured when they are positioned as experts and their knowledge, practices, and language are recognized as educational and when teachers take a learner's stance, as Julia and Mary Jade did.

Establishing supportive relationships with principals, by providing rationales for classroom practice rooted in the literature, explaining how standards are addressed, and sharing the results of effective work, is key. When teachers explain their work and demonstrate links to mandated standards, they answer some administrator questions before they can be asked. In sum, relationships and taking the time—a lot of time—to build them are part of the work of culturally relevant teaching. Allowing time to create relationships, protecting those relationships and the needed time, and advocating for both are critical.

Lesson #4: Engage with Young Children Around Complex Issues

Experiences

Contrary to what some of us may have learned (and taught) early in our careers about young children's concrete and egocentric thinking combined with the common misperceptions that they must be protected from so-called provocative issues, the young children in the PDCRT classrooms were given opportunities to grapple with complex, politically fraught topics, including immigration, racial discrimination, identity, and fairness and equity, and historical events such as the Civil Rights Movement and presidential elections. Dyads found this to be critical to the development of a critically conscious classroom.

Children of every age in every dyad demonstrated the capacity to engage, ask questions, and think deeply and empathically without trivializing complex issues when given the opportunity and support to do so. For example, in our interviews of PDCRT participants, one of the board members highlighted a school–community march for peace linked to current issues that was organized by Alicia and Bilal's school to commemorate Dr. Martin Luther King Day. As she explained:

> Just having the children participate … sometimes that's so remote for them, they're hearing it but how intense are the conversations that they're having that they're really taking it in. But then to actually participate in a march I think spoke volumes to *them* … . You were in it. You were doing it. So that's why that was just so powerful for me.

Other teachers also skillfully scaffolded children's critical abilities. Patricia interacted with her student Julia playfully as they both pronounced her name correctly in Spanish. Then she extended the learning to action by modeling what Julia could say when her name is mispronounced and by urging parents to insist on the Spanish pronunciation of their children's names. Alicia engaged with her students in challenging discussions of race, racism, and colorism in the context of their studies of Celia Cruz, Tito Puente, and Maya Angelou.

Perspectives and Action Steps

In order to implement culturally relevant teaching as a foundational ideology, it is important for educators to know the children and listen to them, identifying culturally significant projects that can provide opportunities for learning, for addressing standards, and for critical talk and taking action. Teachers can provide scaffolding, highlight relevant issues interrogating equity, make personal connections, and teach needed skills in engaging, often physically active, and authentic work like the march for peace, Patricia's playful name lesson, and Alicia's inquiries into well-known African American and Latinx people. What is key is teachers' ability to take a risk and, well prepared, start interactions and more complex inquiries that sometimes move in unpredictable and challenging directions with young children. As teachers organize ways for children to use their new knowledge to impact their school or community, children will experience their ability—alone or collectively—to question and create change. At times these topics will be introduced by the children so it is the teacher's responsibility to respond, often by inviting children to discuss them in school, to listen, accept what they say, and move them to understanding and action. Teacher educators sometimes have to act as buffers or mediators between their risk-taking dyad partners on the one hand and colleagues and administrators on the other, whether the issue is "appropriateness" or challenging content for young children.

Lesson #5: Center Teachers, Children, and Families of Color; Decenter Whiteness

Experiences

As a project grounded in promoting leadership from educators of Color and working to decenter Whiteness, we saw both progress and the depth of that challenge, recognizing the hold of White supremacy on all of us in different ways. The original directors, White teacher educators, committed to the plan to step back at the end of the first PDCRT cohort, drawing leadership for future cohorts from the dyads and board members of Color. In addition, as mentioned earlier, the initial PDCRT goal to build leadership within the NCTE among early childhood educators of Color continues to be met as past and present PDCRT cohort members (now completing its third two-year cohort and planning the fourth) serve as leaders on NCTE's Executive Committee, Elementary Section Steering Committee, Latinx Caucus, and Board of Trustees of the Research Foundation; mentors and fellows in NCTE's Cultivating New Voices Among Scholars of Color; and as the leadership of NCTE's Early Childhood Education Assembly. Members of the first cohort and subsequent ones also moved into leadership in their schools, districts, and universities: a principal; a Director of Diversity, Equity, and Poverty; grade-level chairs; an Equity Through Excellence Education Officer; a district Language Arts specialist; a chair of a university's diversity council; and members of school leadership teams, to name a few.

The intentional selection of readings that center the histories, experiences, and perspectives of people of Color was also key to learning to decenter Whiteness. Some of the joint readings of the cohorts, included Alexander's *The New Jim Crow* (2010) and King and Swartz's *The Afrocentric Praxis of Teaching for Freedom* (2016) plus Coates' *Between the World and Me* (2015). Together these readings challenged Eurocratic narratives (those officially sanctioned and systemic narratives stemming from Euro-American worldviews) about race and racism in the U. S. by presenting Afrocentric narratives that helped us talk about the Eurocratic nature of schooling and the potential for African-centered teaching. This led to fruitful and sometimes difficult conversations as previously unquestioned practices, perspectives, and identities were challenged. There was no single way that we negotiated these; we listened and talked; interrogated our own practice, and most important, together explored, experimented with, and analyzed classroom practices for the extent to which they were actually culturally relevant, antiracist, and Afro-centric pedagogies. In our retrospective interviews, several participants noted that by committing to these kinds of readings and discussion spaces, the project provided them with a "safe space" for contradicting conventions that normalized White experiences and perspectives. Another participant explained that the trusting relationships within and across dyads created a space where challenges could be raised and met openly and with support.

The dyad work described in this book was led by educators who centered their teaching on the languages, cultures, and histories of their students and their families, countering deficit perspectives typically engendered by the White Gaze and rejecting many of the developmental norms and constraints established by the early childhood literature. Patricia and Kindel, for example, were unflagging advocates for the Latinx children's languages and communities through pedagogy and Patricia's compilation of authentic, bilingual assessment data for children to counter the testing conducted in English by outside school personnel. Similarly, Mary Jade and Julia foregrounded and were able to share with classroom teachers Latinx mothers' knowledge, expertise, and commitments to their children's education. Alicia demonstrated to her supervisor and dyad partner Bilal how she could develop multiple inquiry projects with her second-graders grounded in the languages, histories, and cultures of the children. Chinyere and Crystal highlighted the knowledge and successes of the second-graders in Chinyere's class to the children themselves and to other constituents as the children researched their own heritages.

Perspectives and Action Steps

Listen to *and hear* educators of Color—colleagues, children, families, community members, and professional educators through their writing—to grapple with issues of inequity and discrimination, then take responsibility for using that knowledge to change policies and practices. White educators working alongside educators of Color have an important role to play by insisting that their institutions acknowledge structural oppressions and systematic modes of sustaining White dominance and take steps to overhaul them.

Continual self and institutional reflection on progress—or lack of it—toward decentering Whiteness is an important part of the process of transforming thinking and pedagogy. As one PDCRT teacher who was also a board member noted, "[W]e had to explore our own beliefs. We had to explore our own prejudices and be honest about it in order for us to move into this work." The opportunities that the project offered to put our evolving ideas into practice with children and families and to critique them together generated growth and learning for all of us. In addition, as emphasized in Lesson #4 about challenging Eurocratic early childhood assumptions, reflection on and critique of Eurocratic early childhood practices can raise questions about the hidden racism inherent, for example, in the concept of developmentally appropriate practice, which was originally developed with and for White children as representing the norm of maturational growth.

Lesson #6: Teach Literacy as a Social and Cultural Practice

Experiences

Each dyad effectively grounded their work in an understanding of literacy as a social and cultural practice of meaning making and by valuing and forefronting the languages and cultural practices of the children, families, and communities. Children and adults working with all the dyads read and wrote texts that reflected their thoughts and lives. In preschool and primary classrooms across the project, children engaged in dramatic play and acted in plays. Children in Chinyere's classroom wrote and performed scripts, while others wrote songs and raps that reflected in their content and style the historically valued performances they experienced in their lives. With Chinyere, students shared information about their home and heritage languages in presentations to other classes and family audiences. Similarly, Patricia's preschoolers made books that reflected their communities and highlighted and honored their names. In Alicia's classroom children studied an African American poet and listened to her recorded poetry and also studied the lives and music of famous Latinx musicians. In Alicia's and others' classrooms, children wrote questions and interviewed parents and community members. Overall, the children read a range of texts and used a range of artifacts and digital media; some took photographs and reflected on them, as did the mothers' group. Working with Julia and Mary Jade, Latinx mothers read children's books, not as part of instruction in the "correct" way to read to children but as part of discussions about the languages and content. In every PDCRT classroom, the children wrote in their home languages—including African American Language, Spanish, and languages indigenous to Latin America—often while translanguaging or code-meshing with forms of English.

Perspectives and Action Steps

In the process of implementing culturally relevant activities, teachers can pay attention to children and families and voices from their communities as well as their historically valued and contemporary cultures, then curricularize what they are learning. That means using children and families' interests, expertise, and languages as the foundation of curriculum. Following children's questions, providing for multiple forms of literacy as ways for children to learn and express their knowledge authentically and actively, and using multiple means of communication are possible strategies. Teachers can prepare children to succeed on standardized measures through experiences of reading, writing, listening to, and speaking about topics compelling for children while also using more authentic, potentially less biased, and culturally relevant means of assessment.

Lesson #7: Learn from Families

Experiences

Foundational to our work was a belief in families informing curriculum and coming into the classroom not just to help teachers but to teach children and for teachers to learn from them. This commitment to learning from and with families took different forms in different settings. Patricia and Kindel reflected on deeply rooted community practices of translanguaging (using all of a child's languages as resources), warm demanding (a style combining high expectations and strong support), and *consejos* (traditional sayings; family lessons) in their classroom interactions. In Alicia's and Chinyere's classrooms, translanguaging was also used as a powerful tool for communicating. In both classrooms, family members were interviewed by their children about their childhoods and school experiences as well as their experiences as immigrants. And Chinyere also conducted home visits to chat over coffee and learn about parents' concerns and questions. In all four settings, the families were positioned as experts, teachers at home and in the classroom too.

In Mary Jade and Julia's work with Latinx mothers, the dyad neither critiqued nor dictated what they thought the mothers should do. Meeting three times a month to discuss Latinx children's books, go on field trips, and talk about issues important to them, the group provided a space where the mothers felt comfortable talking while Mary Jade and Julia listened and responded, following the mothers' lead and learning from them. In the process, the mothers learned that their perspectives and questions were valued and that they had a significant place in the life of the school. As Julia remarked in our interview with her, "Hopefully as the student goes through the system [the parent] can go on with confidence of 'I have a question.' 'I have a right to say this is not good for my child. And it's ok for me to say that that's not right for my child.'"

Perspectives and Action Steps

The PDCRT dyads demonstrated that it is critical for teachers and teacher educators to discuss innovative ways to work with families that value their contributions in creating culturally relevant classrooms. This means getting to know them, establishing trust, and understanding that work with families begins with their goals for their children, not ours. This work may include speaking their language(s), taking a learner's stance, learning about their expertise, sharing goals, seeking their input formally and informally, making home visits, providing them with tools for advocating for their children such as helping them understand how certain school procedures work and sharing ways to approach and speak to school personnel. Parents can be integrated into "triads" instead of "dyads," creating more formal relationships. Such collaborative groups would include family members, teachers, and teacher educators. Equally important is the long-term job of hiring teachers like Julia from the same cultural/ language group who can bring an insider's knowledge and advocacy to a project. The importance of taking time and thought to cultivate relationships with families to help them understand our work as we work with them cannot be overstated.

Lesson #8: Study Together to Develop a Critical Perspective

Experiences

From the beginning, we knew that the work of PDCRT had to be more than the implementation of activities, even those that challenged the standard colonizing curriculum, and that there was a need for joint study linked with the development of a critical perspective. Thus, together we read works by Souto-Manning (2013), Ladson-Billings (2014), and Delpit (2012) in addition to those mentioned above and discussed them in blogs and during virtual and face-to-face meetings. As noted in the interviews, often there was not as much time as we would have liked to discuss them in depth. Nonetheless, the infusion of conceptual writing in the books and reflective discussion prompted by classroom experiences too helped us nurture a critical perspective and understandings of the broader contexts of the past and present movements toward pedagogical and societal change.

Collaborative discussions of readings that challenged the thinking of both teachers and teacher educators leveled the field and contributed to the development of mutual mentorships. Dyad members realized that, in some ways, prior to PDCRT they had already been implementing culturally relevant pedagogies that they could now name as such. They also realized that, at times, they had been merely skimming the surface. Group study across dyads helped to reveal this and to deepen our knowledge. As a result, dyads were inspired to extend these pedagogies in new ways, becoming more intentional in their use as well as advocating for them within and beyond their schools. For example, Chinyere's book group with colleagues spread the message of PDCRT to her whole school. Readings gave theoretical and historical teeth to teachers' arguments when they articulated their work to administrators. And once PDCRT participants began to read with the project, they went on to read after the project while collaborating to write in peer-reviewed journals and to publish books and present at national conferences.

Perspectives and Action Steps

It is important to recognize teaching as intellectual and political work and then to provide time and opportunities for teachers and teacher educators to read, reflect, present, think, and act collaboratively, learning to work together from a critical stance. In the process, they can identify elements of their work that already challenge the monocultural and monolingual status quo as they deepen their knowledge and take risks to generate new and innovative strategies. Virtual meetings, blogs, joint attendance at conferences, as well as face-to-face discussions, can all contribute to this kind of collaborative growth.

Lesson #9: Develop Equitable Assessments

Experiences

As the project progressed, we came to better understand the complex task we had set ourselves of helping children succeed on standardized measures while challenging those measures as discriminatory. Though assessment was not highlighted in PDCRT's formal goals, it was a key theme in the dyads' description of their work in this volume.

Strong examples of culturally relevant and culturally supportive assessment can be found across dyads. For example, Patricia assessed children as emerging bilinguals and used portfolios including anecdotal notes, observation checklists, formative assessments, formal assessment, recordings of informal conversations, photos, and samples of children's work as part of an authentic assessment process to reveal the knowledge and skills of children such as Santiago. Chinyere used interviews, checklists, and children's products as well to provide insights into their learning. Alicia and Bilal created culturally relevant texts and assessment materials that ultimately resulted in students' powerful growth, as demonstrated on the conventional and dominant literacy assessment by Fountas and Pinnell (2010) used in their school.

In all four settings, the dyads worked against the oppressive power of standardized, high-stakes, official, biased assessments to counter damage—at least for a school year—that traditional assessments inflict on children and families by failing to provide a true picture of children's literacy abilities.

Perspectives and Action Steps

It is important for teachers and teacher educators to take a stand to advocate for sustaining children's languages, literacies, histories, and heritage while preparing them for standardized assessments *and* challenging these assessments. For this PDCRT cohort, this meant supplementing official assessments with multiple, more useful, valid, and culturally relevant measures which could not yet be used as official alternatives but represent a step forward in identifying potential alternatives. While there is little in the literature on culturally relevant assessment, many teachers use such assessments already and explicitly identifying them can be part of the process of creating culturally relevant pedagogies. Other innovative assessment strategies can be gleaned from the literature and the work of colleagues; many more will be generated by practice. Documenting and disseminating information about such assessments helps the field make progress toward addressing this challenge.

How Can We Move Toward Culturally Sustaining Pedagogies?

The PDCRT project is driven by a commitment to changing an unjust, Euro-dominant status quo in pedagogy, policy, and practice. Through the development, implementation, and documentation of teaching practices, dyads and board members worked to stay true to the theoretical constructs of culturally relevant teaching as outlined by Ladson-Billings (1995), which meant that they focused on developing students' cultural competence, critical consciousness, and achievement. It was not until after this cohort's two-year participation in the PDCRT project that many of us began reading about Paris and Alim's (2017b) conceptualization of culturally *sustaining* pedagogy, which is grounded primarily in work done in secondary education. We wondered how we could move our work toward their tenets as we continued to explore the implications of this work in early childhood classrooms.

As this book's editors note in Chapter One, the theory of culturally sustaining pedagogy was constructed as part of a "loving critique" (Paris & Alim, 2014, p. 85) of Ladson-Billings' articulation of culturally relevant pedagogy and an attempt to "shift the term, stance, and practice of asset pedagogies toward more explicitly pluralist outcomes" (p. 87). CSP moves beyond culturally relevant pedagogies to center the cultural and linguistic riches of children of Color, their cultural dexterity in moving within and across cultures, not as a means to meet the colonized and colonizing objectives of education today, but as the foundations of disruptive and transformative curriculum and teaching. We see this as constituting an overhaul of the institution of education through "explicit resistances that embrace cultural pluralism and cultural equality" (Paris, 2012, p. 95) as the norm in schooling and in society. Paris and Alim (2017b) argue that "CSP, then, is necessary to honor, value, and center the rich and varied practices of communities of color, *and*, is a necessary pedagogy for helping shape access to power in a changing nation" (p. 6). Recapped below are characteristic features of CSP provided by Paris and Alim (2017a) and laid out in Chapter One:

1. A critical centering on dynamic community languages, valued practices, and knowledges [that must be] centered meaningfully.
2. Student and community agency and input (community accountability).
3. Historicized content and instruction [that] connect[s] present learning to the histories
4. of racial, ethnic, and linguistic communities, and to the histories of neighborhoods and cities, and the histories of the larger states and nation-states that they are a part of.
5. A capacity to contend with internalized oppressions (and counter messages and systems that suggest that marginalized students and families are the problem and value White, middle-class, monolingual, monocultural values above all else).
6. An ability to curricularize these features in learning settings.

Paris and Alim also emphasize that these pedagogical features are not enough. In a 2019 presentation, Paris explained that they must go hand-in-hand with a willingness "to resist and refuse when school, district, and state curriculum, policies, and practices reinforce these false and damaging beliefs in superiority" (Paris, 2019).

As can be seen in Figure 6.2, the work of the dyads described in the preceding chapters consists primarily of elements representing features #1 through #4 and are examples of #5, the curricularization of those features, that is, honoring and extending those features through normalizing them in the curriculum. We see these PDCRT activities as intentional efforts to "resist and refuse" normalized Eurocratic curriculum, policies, and practices. However, because they were implemented during the course of two school years, the degree to which the dyad work is actually sustaining is not yet clear. We are left to ask: Will multiculturalism, multilingualism, and criticality be sustained in the dyad schools, students' lives, and surrounding communities when these committed teachers and administrator leave? If not, why? And without committed educators, what will it take for the ideology underlying this work to take hold as foundational to institutions? With those questions in mind, the work of PDCRT—which is culturally relevant and an important contribution to literature on pedagogy in early literacy and early childhood education—moves "forward with love" (Paris & Alim, 2014, p. 95) toward culturally sustaining pedagogy, toward offering "education for the human soul" (Cooper, 1892). We move forward, however, with sober hope (Bell, 1992), a kind of hope that "allows people to see the realism of the situation and to not expect miraculous, uncomplicated changes" (Boutte, 2015, p. 89). We feel confident that the work of PDCRT plays an important role in the movement toward cultural and linguistic pluralism as a pedagogical norm, recognizing that this involves challenging and transforming the monocultural and monolingual goals of our Eurocratic systems of education.

When studying Figure 6.2, it is also important to note that, while some practices may be aligned with principles of CSP, they do not constitute a template to replicate. Instead, they were co-constructed by the dyads and their students and families and

Features of CSP (Paris & Alim, 2017b)	*CSP features evident in PDCRT work*
1. A critical centering on dynamic community languages, valued practices, and knowledges [that must be] centered meaningfully;	Honoring community language practices & parenting strategies when teaching
	Supporting children's translanguaging & reflecting translanguaging in the classroom environment
	Grounding mothers' group & other school–parent interactions in their languages, practices, knowledge, & concerns, not "teaching them how to"
	Selecting & creating books reflecting children's languages, cultures, races, & interests & discussing them with parents
	Valuing & organizing children's study of revered figures in
	community, of sports teams, popular culture, music & literacies, heritages & countries of origin
	Integrating parents as participants into learning activities
2. Student and community agency and input (community accountability);	Engaging family members as active participants in school community
	Communicating consistently & constructively about children's strengths & challenges with family
	Providing parents with resources & preparation for
	school encounters with other teachers, administrators, special services teams
	Using multiple means, modalities, and sites for communicating with families & for families to use
	Creating literal & figurative space for families in schools &
	curriculum
	Teaching to students' strengths and possibilities for growth not perceived developmental level
	Working from ecological, contextualized view of learning & development that understands them as embedded in family/cultural/sociohistorical contexts
	Establishing *confianza*, a community value/practice based on mutual respect
	Organizing children's research & presentations to community on family assets & histories
	Organizing children's interviews of family members
	Providing multiple ways for children to demonstrate learning
	Using authentic, contextualized, translanguaged, culturally relevant assessments
	Preparing children for standardized assessments

Features of CSP (Paris & Alim, 2017b)	*CSP features evident in PDCRT work*
3. Historicized content and instruction [that] connect[s] present learning to the histories of racial, ethnic, and linguistic communities, and to the histories of neighborhoods and cities, and the histories of the larger states and nation-states that they are a part of;	Disrupting colonized history of school relationships with families & communities Welcoming families regardless of immigration status Organizing children's research into family histories, heritage countries, languages, music, & literacies Creating opportunities for children & families to discuss racism, immigration, fairness, & justice Introducing community sites to children and families through field trips that connect with family experiences Creating multilingual curricula that reflect children's families & communities
4. A capacity to contend with internalized oppressions [and counter messages and systems that suggest that marginalized students and families are the problem and value White, middle-class, monolingual, monocultural values above all else];	Insisting on & modeling correct pronunciation of children's and families' names Confronting English-only school policies and discourses & furthering parents' abilities to understand and challenge them Strengthening mothers' abilities to advocate for children Standing up to biased assessments and providing alternatives Advocating for children & families with colleagues & administrators; countering deficit assumptions Fostering children's ability to speak back to others' deficit perspectives of them Validating children's interests, questions, expertise, & heritages by centering them in the curriculum Providing opportunities for teachers, teacher educators, and students to engage in inquiry, debate, research, discussion, analysis, questions, & arguments Fostering children's positive understandings of race, heritage, language, and modeling language to discuss those issues with others Fostering children's autonomy & choice, including with student-led lessons Fostering colleagues' understanding of culturally relevant teaching & abilities to use it by offering and providing professional development
5. An ability to curricularize these features in learning settings (Paris & Alim, 2017b).	The examples above represent ways the dyads curricularized features #1–#4 during the time they were in the PDCRT project.

FIGURE 6.2 Features of CSP and Summary of CSP Features from Chapters 2–5.

grew out of their experiences together, infused with their cultures, in their specific schools and communities, at particular social-historical conjunctures. Thus, while some practices, for example teaching "to the potential and not the perceived developmental level of our children" (Díaz & Flores, 2001, p. 31), as described in Chapter Three, may apply to all settings as challenges to Eurocratic early childhood practice, the multiple ways it can be implemented will depend on each educator's experiences, students, families, and context. Other examples such as the use of *consejos* in Chapter Two were very specific to the teacher's culture and that of the children in her class and can provide inspiration and insights about ways in which the cultures of teachers, students, and families can be foregrounded in classroom work.

With these thoughts in mind about the characteristics of CSP, the potentially tenuous nature of the work, the importance of avoiding formulas, and the work of four PDCRT dyads reported in this book, we consider what we would need to do in order to move toward culturally sustaining pedagogies. To do so, we revisit Paris and Alim's (2017a) questions paraphrased in Chapter One (questions 1–4 below) and we add additional questions drawing on our PDCRT work (questions 5–10 below). We offer these questions to provoke self-reflection as we and other educators seek sustainability:

1. How can our pedagogies be culturally sustaining and what is it we seek to sustain?
2. How does our answer to that question influence what we decide to read, write, speak, and teach?
3. What and who are the sources of knowledge we must be in critical conversation with?
4. How are we critically learning within communities? (Paris & Alim, 2017a)
5. When is our teaching a supportive, culturally relevant *moment in time* and not necessarily sustaining of multiculturalism and multilingualism in the lives of students and their communities or sustainable in our own institution? What will it take for our culturally relevant work to be sustaining and sustainable?
6. Can one teacher's practice lead to sustaining culture and language in the life of a child? In the life of a school? In the life of a community?
7. When committed educators leave a school setting, how can the commitment be sustained? What does it take for educational settings to avoid slipping back into Eurocratic practices that silence and degrade the work toward normalized multilingualism and multiculturalism?
8. What additional knowledge, shifts in understanding and ideology, and risk-taking actions are required of educators individually? Collaboratively?
9. What changes are required institutionally and what are the drawbacks of institutionalization?
10. What might schools and classrooms, especially those with young children, look and be like if culturally sustaining pedagogies were fully implemented?

As mentioned earlier, at the core of this work is a willingness to identify and give up/dismantle unjust power structures, which brings us to a final set of self-reflective questions. These are relevant to all educators but imperative for those of us who are White—including this chapters' authors—who "must be willing to give up the false and damaging belief that who we are (and the unjust power that may come with our identities), that what our norms and beliefs are, somehow deserve more attention in schools" (Paris, 2019). We ask:

1. In what specific ways am I (or is my school) perpetuating and fostering "linguistic, literate, and cultural pluralism as a part of schooling for positive social transformation and revitalization" (Paris & Alim, 2017a), recognizing that, for this to truly be a part of schooling, it must be seen and enacted as foundational, daily, and the norm?

   - What has to happen in my classroom and my institution for that to occur?
   - What barriers do I see to making this happen?
   - What do I need to do next to move us toward that goal?

2. In what ways am I willing to divest from "the ways whiteness castes normed practices and bodies as superior … what spaces am I willing to relinquish to make necessary space for centering others, other life ways in [my] classrooms and schools?" (Paris, 2019)
3. In what specific ways will I "resist and refuse when school, district, and state curriculum, policies, and practices reinforce these false and damaging beliefs in superiority?" (Paris, 2019)

Conclusion

In summary, participants in the PDCRT project who shared their work in this book began with a sense of excitement and urgency about the need to challenge unjust educational practices and institutions, especially in moments marked by a strengthening of the progenitors of racism, anti-Semitism, anti-Muslim, and anti-immigrant, monocultural movements and the intersecting neoliberal project[2] (Sleeter, 2018). While challenges emerged along the way, these PDCRT collaborations ultimately renewed and energized these participants and left us more knowledgeable, confident, and courageous. In the retrospective interviews, teachers spoke about finding their voice and feeling empowered, knowing they were no longer "just teachers," moving beyond being "star struck" when working with university faculty, some of whom had written the articles and books they were reading. They were inspired by their PDCRT colleagues to work more collaboratively with parents and community members. Teacher educators explained that they had new-found credibility with their university students as they advocated for and implemented pedagogies that reflected the lives, heritages, and cultures of marginalized children, families, and communities. A board member who is also a teacher educator noted, "Those collaborations have moved my thinking in monumental ways as I consider what's possible in developing more equitable educational practices."

We began this chapter with Carmen Tisdale's words, "If not me, then who?" Carmen spoke them in the context of explaining how culturally relevant pedagogies "gave me life in teaching; my children needed it." They reflect her belief that the responsibility lies with her and with every other teacher and teacher educator dedicated to overturning an unjust status quo. It is a status quo in which children of Color are often denied opportunities for success, not because of their own lives and abilities but because of teaching and living in a system that negates those lives, histories, languages, and heritage in "a saga of linguistic and cultural loss [that] has had and continues to have devastating effects for the access and achievement of students and communities of color in U.S. schools" (Paris, 2012, p. 95). It is a kind of teaching that matters for every child as we work together not just to teach in culturally relevant ways for a day, a week, a month, or a year but as sustained, that is, as foundational to the educational institutions in which we work. "If not us, then who?"

Notes

1 Anonymous quotes describing project goals are taken from the retrospective interviews with PDCRT participants.

2 Neoliberalism is the latest version of our capitalist economic system that fosters individual needs over community, privatization over government guarantee, and provision of services, choice over rights.

References

Alexander, M. (2010). *The new Jim Crow: Mass incarceration the age of colorblindness*. New York, NY: New Press.

Baines, J., Tisdale, C., & Long, S. (2018). *"We've been doing it your way long enough": Choosing the culturally relevant classroom*. New York, NY: Teachers College Press.

Bell, D. (1992). *Faces at the bottom of the well: The permanence of racism*. New York, NY: Basic Books.

Boutte, G. S. (2015). *Educating African American students: And how are the children?*New York, NY: Routledge.

Coates, T. (2015). *Between the world and me*. New York, NY: Spiegel and Grau.

Cooper, A. J. (1892). The higher education of women. In M. H. Washington (Ed.), *A voice from the south* (pp. 48–79). Oxford: Oxford University Press.

Delpit, L. (2012). *"Multiplication is for White people": Raising expectations for other people's children*. New York, NY: The New Press.

Díaz, E., & Flores, B. (2001). Teacher as sociocultural, sociohistorical mediator: Teaching to the potential. In M. Reyes & J. J. Halcón (Eds.), *The best for our children: Critical perspectives on literacy for Latino students* (pp. 29–47). New York, NY: Teachers College Press.

Fountas, I. C., & Pinnell, G. S. (2010). *Fountas & Pinnell benchmark assessment system 1, grades K–2, levels A–N*. Portsmouth, NH: Heinemann.

King, J. E., & Swartz, E. E. (2014). *Re-membering history in student and teacher learning: An Afrocentric culturally informed praxis*. New York, NY: Routledge.

King, J. E., & Swartz, E. E. (2016). *The Afrocentric praxis of teaching for freedom: Connecting culture to learning*. New York, NY: Routledge.

Ladson-Billings, G. (1995). But that's just good teaching! The case for culturally relevant pedagogy. *Theory into Practice*, 34, 159–165.

Ladson-Billings, G. (2012). Through a glass darkly: The persistence of race in education research & scholarship. *Educational Researcher*, 41, 115–120.

Ladson-Billings, G. (2014). Culturally relevant pedagogy 2.0: a.k.a. the remix. *Harvard Educational Review*, *84*, 74–84.

Ladson-Billings, G. (2017). The (r)evolution will not be standardized: Teacher education, hip hop pedagogy, and culturally relevant pedagogy 2.0. In D. Paris & H. S. Alim (Eds.), *Culturally sustaining pedagogies: Teaching and learning for justice in a changing world* (pp. 141–156). New York, NY: Teachers College Press.

Morrison, T. (1998, March). *From an interview on Charlie Rose*. Public Broadcasting Service. Retrieved from http://www.youtube.com/watch?v=F4vIGvKpT1c

Paris, D. (2012). Culturally sustaining pedagogy: A needed change in stance, terminology, and practice. *Educational Researcher*, 41(3), 93–97.

Paris, D. (2019). *Must we sustain? CSP in the current moment forward* [Power Point slides]. Center for the Education and Equity of African American Students, College of Education, University of South Carolina.

Paris, D., & Alim, H. S. (2014). What are we seeking to sustain through culturally sustaining pedagogy? A loving critique forward. *Harvard Educational Review*, 84, 85–100.

Paris, D., & Alim, H. S. (2017a). *Author interview by Larry Ferlazzo: Culturally sustaining pedagogies*. Retrieved from http://blogs.edweek.org/teachers/classroom_qa_with_larry_ferlazzo/2017/07/author_interview_culturally_sustaining_pedagogies.html?r=604476754.

Paris, D., & Alim, H. S. (2017b). *Culturally sustaining pedagogies: Teaching and learning for justice in a changing world*. New York, NY: Teachers College Press.

Sleeter, C. (2018). Multicultural education past, present, and future: Struggles for dialog and power sharing. *International Journal of Multicultural Education*, 20, 5–20.

Souto-Manning, M. (2013). *Multicultural teaching in the early childhood classroom Approaches, strategies, and tools, preschool–2nd grade*. New York, NY: Teachers College Press.

EPILOGUE

The ideas expressed in this book are like a cipher. A cipher[1] is a culturally sustaining practice that involves people (usually young people) interacting in a circular fashion sharing ideas—communal and personal. Ciphers have been utilized frequently in hip hop culture through dance, rap, and dialogue—both formally and informally (Emdin, 2013). The practice of sharing in a cipher was influenced by the cultural group, the Five Percent Nation of Gods and Earths, who historically has been known to build and share ideas in ciphers (Peterson, 2013). The practice of forming a cipher to build, to create a space, to contribute, and to add on comes from a lineage of African and Indigenous practices of families and communities coming together to share and to celebrate and honor voices, ideas, and stories (Freire, 2018; Hill & Petchauer, 2013). We offer this idea of a cipher as a space through which we and our readers can **add on** as we all create opportunities to "constantly challenge ourselves and others to 'show and prove,' to do pedagogical work that allows us to escape with our souls" (Alim & Haupt, 2017, pp. 171–172).

The family tree (Figure 1.2) described in Chapter One is one way our work reflects the cipher in the way that it honors the people, places, and movements that inspire us, growing and changing as we continue to read, experience, and reflect, individually and communally. Similarly, we form ciphers in our everyday work as we create communal spaces for ourselves, our staff, and students. For example, in Bilal's school, each class comes together in a cipher for a daily morning meeting, where all students gather in a circle to share and connect with one another before the day begins. Crystal begins each university class by gathering students in a circle for community-building rituals—for example, responding to a prompt asking students to check in with themselves about how they are feeling. At the beginning of each fall semester, as teacher candidates are about to begin their student teaching internship, Kindel and other university faculty she works with form a circle and ask everyone including faculty, to "walk their story," collectively sharing the experiences and the values that have shaped them individually. Thus, as have other educators, we borrow the concept of cipher in our day-to-day work, but also to urge readers to engage in work that balances "individuality … with the increasingly marginalized values of community, collaboration, and representing … supporting individual[s] while rebuilding the circle around [them]" (Kuttner & White-Hammond, 2013, p. 46).

We invite readers to use this book as a foundation for creating their own spaces for this kind of collaboration and growth. In support of that work, it may be helpful to create your own Family Tree to represent the dynamic, living, growing foundation of your work, so we provide a blank Family Tree in Appendix A so that you can craft your own path to culturally sustaining pedagogies. In the tradition of our ancestors and our youth, we ask you to please, add on to the cipher.

Peace,
Kindel, Crystal, and Bilal

Note

1 Readers may see the word 'cipher' spelled in different ways (e.g., cypher, cypha). This reflects the creative alteration of traditional word spellings common in hip hop writing/journalism.

References

Alim, H. S., & Haupt, A. (2017). Reviving soul (s) with Afrikaaps: Hip Hop as culturally sustaining pedagogy in South Africa. In D. Paris & S. Alim (Eds.), *Culturally sustaining pedagogies: Teaching and learning for justice in a changing world* (pp. 157–174). New York, NY: Teachers College Press.

Emdin, C. (2013). Pursuing the pedagogical potential of the pillars of hip-hop through sciencemindedness. *The International Journal of Critical Pedagogy*, 4(3), 83–99.

Freire, P. (2018). *Pedagogy of the oppressed*. New York, NY: Bloomsbury Publishing USA.

Hill, M. L., & Petchauer, E. (Eds.). (2013). *Schooling hip-hop: Expanding hip-hop based education across the curriculum*. New York, NY: Teachers College Press.

Kuttner, P. J., & White-Hammond, M. (2014). Building the cipher: Fulfilling the promise of hip hop for liberation. In C. Malone & G. Martinez, Jr (Eds.), *The organic globalizer: Hip hop, political development, and movement culture* (pp. 43–55). New York, NY: Bloomsbury Publishing USA.

Peterson, J. B. (2013). Rewriting the remix: College composition and the educational elements of hip-hop. In M. L. Hill & E. Petchauer (Eds.), *Schooling hip-hop: Expanding hip-hop based education across the curriculum* (pp. 47–60). New York, NY: Teachers College Press.

APPENDIX

FIGURE A.1 Blank Family Tree: Add to the Cipher

A blank family tree template is available for download as an eResource at www.routledge.com/9780815363750

INDEX

Locators in *italics* refer to figures and those in **bold** to tables.